# Cunard's Queens Revealed

## The Evolution of Six Great Passenger Ships

David L. Williams

Ian Allan

PUBLISHING

First published 2011

ISBN 978 0 7110 3531 7

© David L. Williams 2011

Published by Ian Allan Publishing
an imprint of Ian Allan Publishing Ltd, Hersham, Surrey KT12 4RG.
Printed in England by Ian Allan Printing Ltd, Hersham, Surrey KT12 4RG.

Visit the Ian Allan Publishing website at *www.ianallanpublishing.com*
Distributed in the United States of America and Canada by
BookMasters Distribution Services.

# Contents

**FRONT COVER** A trials view of the *Queen Mary 2* making a hard turn to starboard, an exercise designed to test her stability as well as to measure her turning circle. The distinctive twin white exhausts aft on Deck 13 give her a balanced profile. While they effectively make the *QM2* a three-stack ship, the adoption of the twin exhausts spared her from any attempt to replicate the style of the original *Queen Mary* with three more conventional funnels of descending height. *Cunard*

**BACK COVER** The *Queen Mary* at full speed on builders' trials off the island of Arran in April 1936. After the Second World War, the *Queen Mary* and *Queen Elizabeth* usually passed each other in mid-ocean at a combined closing speed of over 70 mph, a close encounter which was a thrilling spectacle to behold for those fortunate enough to have witnessed it.
*National Archives of Scotland*

**PREVIOUS PAGE** Her maiden cruise in December 2007 took the *Queen Victoria* to Rotterdam where she is seen berthed at the Wilhelminakade terminal on a crisp winter's day. *Author*

# Foreword

THE CUNARD QUEENS PAST AND PRESENT are simply the most famous ocean liners ever.

The previous trio – the iconic *Queen Mary, Queen Elizabeth* and *Queen Elizabeth 2* – have not only entered the history books but have created history and their stories are the stuff of legend.

*Queen Mary* was a symbol of Great Britain's emergence from the Depression of the 1930s while *Queen Elizabeth*'s secret dash across the Atlantic, untried and untested in 1940, reads like a story from some great adventure book. Both ships played heroic roles in the war effort and served their country with distinction before becoming the most famous duo on the Atlantic throughout the 1940s and 1950s. What can be said about *Queen Elizabeth 2* that hasn't already? She travelled further than any other ship in history during the course of her remarkable career and carried Cunard through the company's most difficult years. For that we are forever grateful to her.

And today's trio – *Queen Mary 2, Queen Victoria* and *Queen Elizabeth* – are the most famous ships afloat today and comprise the youngest fleet of any operator. It is a fleet that has the most unique and impressive heritage. *Queen Mary 2* is the largest ocean liner ever built and is undoubtedly the grandest and fastest passenger ship afloat today. She reigns supreme on the Atlantic and will continue to do so for many years to come. Her sisters *Queen Victoria* and *Queen Elizabeth* offer their own personality while sharing a common design. Together with *Queen Mary 2* these ships are the three largest Cunarders to have been built for the company and there have been over 250 ships flying the Cunard flag since the company was founded in 1839!

Today's Cunard Queens will journey far into the 21st century and, just like the earlier Queens before them, will enter the history books having created history of their own, contributing to Cunard's long heritage.

I am grateful to David Williams for being the first to combine the stories of our six Queens into one important book. Enjoy and marvel as each of the following pages tells this amazing story, tracking the development of their design and technology as their roles have evolved.

*Peter Shanks*
PRESIDENT AND MANAGING DIRECTOR OF CUNARD LINE
APRIL 2011

The first of Cunard's large, dedicated cruise ships, the *Queen Victoria* is seen on trials in the Adriatic in the autumn of 2007. *Cunard*

# Crossing and Cruising

CUNARD'S RENOWNED QUEENS are not only the most famous ocean liners in the world, as promoted in the company's marketing slogan, but they are also among, if not *the* most successful passenger ships ever placed in service. Instantly recognisable, known by all generations, they have come to epitomise the most supreme standards of maritime transport. Launched at the height of North Atlantic rivalry in the 1930s and continuing in service today, at the very peak of the highly-competitive luxury cruise market, they are, without doubt, the very paragons of ocean travel.

Such plaudits are not bestowed lightly. Many factors in combination have had an influence on the Queens' conspicuous success. Not least there has been the Cunard hallmark which, like other select brand names, stands for excellence in reliability and quality of service. Over the years the Queens themselves have been the beneficiaries of poetic and musical outpourings, countless expressions of admiration and a torrent of accolades pertaining to their size and every facet of their operation. There have probably been more books written about the Queens and more dedicated websites devoted to their history than to any other ships. Thoroughly deserved, the Queens' acclaim is underpinned by their numerous attributes and achievements – their colossal scale, power and speed, their magnificent interiors, their exceptional passenger service, their incomparable accomplishments on the North Atlantic run, their wartime exploits, their sensational world cruises and so on.

Expressed succinctly, Cunard's Queens were and are an amalgam of great British heritage and tradition on the one hand and showcases of cutting-edge interior décor and marine engineering and technology on the other, all encompassed within the framework of the most commercially astute operating philosophy. It has been said that the Queens are truly spectacular ships mechanically, combined with the grandest of resort hotels afloat. All too often, though, the fact that they have also been highly profitable investments tends to be overlooked.

The latest to join the honoured ranks of these extraordinary ships is the new dedicated cruise ship *Queen Elizabeth* which embarked upon her maiden cruise on 12 October 2010, her inauguration commemorating the entry into service of her famous namesake seventy years earlier, in the dark days of the Second World War. The nascence of that great liner in turn celebrated the 100th anniversary of the Cunard Line's inception, when the first sailing from Liverpool to Halifax was made by the small steamship *Britannia*. It was that occasion, on 4 July 1840, which effectively launched Cunard's regular transatlantic mail and passenger service, establishing a mark which was to become permanently associated with shipboard comfort, operational reliability and a standard of cabin service second to none.

Without question, Cunard's legacy of 170 years of successful passenger shipping operation is directly attributable to its long-standing tradition of excellence. The fleet expansion and development made possible by those impeccable standards of performance and the company's corresponding commercial fortunes culminated in 1940. A hundred years after the *Britannia*'s historic voyage, Cunard's crowning achievement was to take the North Atlantic express liner to its zenith in the magnificent *Queen Elizabeth* which for almost sixty years was the largest passenger ship ever built.

With the introduction of the new *Queen Elizabeth*, there are, for only the second time, three Cunard ocean monarchs in service simultaneously, the other two being the *Queen Mary 2* and the *Queen Victoria*. Indeed, five of the six

**ABOVE** Sir Percy Bates, father of the Queens and the architect of the 'Big Ship' policy, the man who was singularly responsible for the realisation of the first two great Queen liners. *Cunard*

Queen liners that have been built remain in existence, for the original *Queen Mary* still lies at Long Beach, California, her post-retirement role of hotel/museum ship entering its 44th year, while, at the time of writing, the iconic *Queen Elizabeth 2* lies at Dubai awaiting her long-term fate.

Each new Queen has entered service amid the greatest of expectations and, though there have been some surprises, they have yet to disappoint. As the standard-bearers of the British Merchant Navy, they are and have been, each in its time, floating manifestations of the wonders of contemporary engineering and technology, champions of modernity in their décor, furnishings and amenities.

Rightly enough, an adoring public romanticises these legendary ships. We perceive them as having an almost mystical quality, largely thanks to highly effective marketing campaigns which have associated them with such concepts as 'ships of dreams', 'floating palaces' or 'cities at sea'. It is all part of the fantasy that many today still want to recreate or experience and it is to Cunard's credit that they have captured those feelings and qualities and perpetuate them today in the most beautiful and elegant surroundings.

But, putting that aside to consider commercial practicalities, each Queen was conceived and commissioned to fulfil a specific, clearly-defined purpose, its service requirements, in respect of function, passenger market and theatre of operations, ultimately dictating its individual design. Viewed in hindsight, it has been Cunard's unwavering adherence to this philosophy that has ensured that each Queen has enjoyed a successful and profitable career, and, no doubt, it will continue likewise for future Queens as they are ordered.

The 'Era of the Queens' began in 1926 when Cunard first considered the possibility of maintaining its weekly North Atlantic express service with only two ships instead of the three on which it then relied. Dubbed the 'Big Ship' policy, it was a vision championed by Sir Percy Elly Bates who took over at the helm, as company Chairman, in 1930. To achieve this radical leap forward, an average service speed of 28.5 knots (32.8 mph) across the 3,000 miles of the Atlantic Ocean was fundamental. At that time, the company's front-line service was operated by the *Mauretania*, *Aquitania* and *Berengaria*, the first named being the fastest of the three as the reigning holder of the Atlantic Blue Riband. That record-breaker's steam turbine engines had a rating of 68,000 shaft horsepower (shp) for a service speed of 25 knots (28.8 mph). To raise this by just 3.5 knots (4.0 mph) required engine power to be more than doubled to 160,000 shp, necessitating a vast power-plant which, in turn, dictated a much larger hull in which to house it. Such ships would be costly to build and operate, consuming a huge quantity of fuel oil. In order to derive an adequate operating revenue to ensure a profitable return on the venture, passenger accommodation for over 2,000 passengers in three classes would have to be provided and ensuring their comfort and satisfaction would be essential if the required percentage of the market was to be secured. There would be magnificent public rooms of a spaciousness and grandeur never before seen, commensurate with the prestigious status of the two ships.

These ingredients comprised the formula from which the scale, dimensions and every other feature of these superlative ships would be calculated. On 27 May 1936, ten years after the dream had begun, the first of the pair, the *Queen Mary*, commenced her maiden voyage to New York from Southampton. And even though, by that date, the world was in the throes of the Great Depression and passenger numbers had halved from their high point of the 1929 season, she fared better than all of her competitors and was judged to be the only large Atlantic liner to turn a profit in those difficult times.

Despite the adverse financial and trading conditions in the mid-1930s, Cunard persisted with its 'Big Ship' programme aided by the British government and committed to build the *Queen Mary*'s running mate. Thus, the *Queen Elizabeth* was ordered as the second of the pair from the same builders in December 1936 for delivery in the company's centenary year.

In the *Queen Elizabeth*, the same broad specification was followed with only cosmetic differences. Benefiting from engineering developments over the intervening years, design modifications resulted in her having a different exterior profile and a more modern look such that the *Queen Mary* and *Queen Elizabeth* may be considered as having been more consorts than sister-ships. Despite these alterations, intrinsically they were equals in a balanced two-ship operation.

Together, for almost twenty years following the end of the Second World War, with few interruptions, they maintained the two-ship weekly express service for which they had been designed. And they were unrivalled, for the other major North Atlantic shipping lines were obliged to join forces to coordinate their schedules in order to offer any competition.

When she emerged some time later, the third Queen, unlike the original pair, was radically different and quite unique, conceived to fulfil a new role that no longer depended exclusively on transatlantic traffic. In recognition of the decline of the scheduled service ocean passenger trade, brought about by a rapid expansion of air travel that had left the traditional liner as something of an anachronism, the 'Queens replacement' project launched in the 1960s finally resulted, after some initial uncertainty, in a single dual-purpose, two-class vessel, the *Queen Elizabeth 2*. Her function would be to spend the Atlantic high season crossing between Southampton and New York while, for the rest of the year, she would operate a programme of luxury cruises, with an annual world cruise as its highlight. Since she would not be required to handle winter North Atlantic weather conditions, the design allowed for some reduction in power and limited her size.

It is interesting to see how the Cunard Chairman of that time, Sir Basil Smallpiece, was incredibly forward-looking in pursuing this radical concept in the face of much traditional opposition. Not only did he correctly perceive the direction in which passenger shipping needed to go but he also anticipated with astonishing accuracy the cruise-shipping scene at the turn of the Millennium. In his address at the Cunard Annual General Meeting in 1966, he said:

LEFT The *Queen Elizabeth*'s First-class Main Lounge taken from a brochure released to promote the Cunard flagship's entry into commercial service. *Bert Moody*

" It is only when we fully grasp the significance of the altered role of passenger shipping in an air-dominated world that we see the dawn of hope for the future.

For then, the new ship [the Queen Elizabeth 2] will no longer be thought of as the last of that great line of large passenger transport vehicles but as the first of an equally great line of ships in the floating hotel or resort business, in which people take a holiday and enjoy themselves. Once it is realised that this role is our future, we are faced no longer with eking out a bare existence in the last decade of passenger sea transport but with the prospect of developing and expanding the vacation industry at sea.

ABOVE Micky Arison, father of the modern Queens and champion of Cunard's great heritage, a man with the almost unique foresight to see a future for the tradition of prestigious passenger ships which has directly resulted in the present generation of great Cunard Queens. *Cunard*

Nevertheless, so different was the ship that Cunard had ordered from the one that had been originally contemplated as a 'Queens replacement', that the company were at pains to stress that she would not be a 'Queen' as then widely understood.

The fact was that, having accepted this dramatic move away from conventional ocean travel, it was possible to exploit engineering developments in the new ship to an extent that would not, otherwise, have been possible.

After battling through inclement times at the start of her career, characterised by technical hiccups, spiralling inflation and economic stagnation along with fast accelerating social change, the *QE2*, as she is fondly known, ultimately established herself over an unparalleled forty-year service career as a highly popular and successful ship. It would be no exaggeration to say that she is probably the best-loved and most warmly remembered cruise liner, a testament to the wisdom behind her unorthodox design concept.

Among the factors which influenced her specification was the requirement that she should be able to transit the Panama Canal, restricting her beam dimensions. Also, the fact that she was not required to endure extreme North Atlantic conditions on a regular basis permitted the adoption of lighter scantlings while another thirty years of marine engineering progress enabled her to achieve the same service speed as the original Queens, with a smaller power-plant and only twin screws. Subsequently, because of the ever-constant pressure to reduce fuel costs as oil prices continued to rise, the *QE2* received life-extending replacement engines as she was approaching her twentieth year of service. Her original steam turbines were substituted by diesel-electric machinery, with few external alterations, and her high standard of performance continued, though achieved with greater efficiency.

It was a widely held view that the *QE2* would be the last of Cunard's giant Queens to be constructed – indeed for a time Cunard marketed her as just that – but, under the stewardship of new owners Carnival Corporation and, notably, promoted by the belief and inspiration of Micky Arison, the parent Company's Chief Executive Officer, the strategists at Cunard set about planning for her replacement, recognising that hers was a winning formula. But there the similarities ended, for the massively impressive *Queen Mary 2*, Cunard's fourth Queen, is different in so many other respects. If the *Queen Elizabeth 2* was an operational hybrid, then the *Queen Mary 2* is more of a structural hybrid. Her hull form, inspired by the last generation of traditional passenger ships, is that of a true deep-water ocean liner while above her main deck she is very much a cruise ship typified by the tiered ranks of outside stateroom balconies.

Stephen Payne, her architect, outlined the fundamental components of his brief for the *Queen Mary 2*:

 *She had to be built of modern materials and by modern methods, able to cross the Atlantic in all weather conditions, and had to earn the same return as if the equivalent money had been spent on [pure] cruise ships.*

Furthermore, she had to be big enough to carry more passengers in top-class accommodation than any previous liner and at least half of those passengers had to have private balconies.

Costing £500 million, the *Queen Mary 2* was built to a demanding specification. Besides requiring her to be far stronger structurally for Atlantic service, it also called for her hull to encompass all the facilities and amenities, at the very highest standard, to fully satisfy the expectations of both cruise and line voyage passengers. Her dimensions were dictated by the service envelope in which she would operate – no higher than the Verrazano Narrows Bridge at New York and no longer than the turning circle off Southampton Docks. The only sacrifice was that her beam would be too great for her to pass through the Panama Canal and so, for the first time, a Cunard world cruise could take passengers around Cape Horn. Designed to re-invent the golden

LEFT The scaled-down reproduction of a section of Doris Zinkheisen's huge decorative mural that was hand-painted on the wall of the *Queen Mary*'s Verandah Grill is the highlight of the Verandah Grill of the new *Queen Elizabeth*. *Author*

age of the passenger liner for a new generation of ocean voyagers and cruise vacationers, she was conceived to sell heritage with a British flavour. As a result, like the *Queen Mary* more than half a century earlier, the *Queen Mary 2* is a showcase of marine engineering wonders and maritime decorative arts. And she has been a success, capable of earning £30,000 an hour.

With the retirement of the *Queen Elizabeth 2*, the *Queen Mary 2* or *QM2*, as her name has been abbreviated, now alone fulfils the company's unique combined Atlantic voyage and cruising mode of operation, but she has far greater passenger capacity than her predecessor. Indeed, she can carry a higher number of passengers in more spacious and better-appointed accommodation than any previous ocean liner. As a consequence of that and her greater number of public spaces, she is a much larger vessel. Thus, her emergence in late 2003 brought the

*Queen Elizabeth*'s 63-year reign as Cunard's largest passenger ship to an end.

Today we are very much in the era of luxury cruise vacations and no-one does them better than Cunard, tapping yet again into more of the Company's long heritage. The standard was set under the flag of the Golden Lion as far back as the 1920s and, immediately after the Second World War, Cunard became the first scheduled-service company to commit a large ocean passenger ship to dedicated cruise service.

Thanks to the cruising boom, today more people than ever before travel by sea partly because, in certain sectors, it is cheaper than it ever was to take a cruise. Arising from that, there are now companies in the cruising mainstream offering high-density, hedonistically active cruise vacations for the mass market, but definitely not Cunard. In stark contrast, Cunard offers a far more

ABOVE The *Queen Elizabeth 2* photographed almost bow on as she completes the turn around the Brambles Bank in the Solent, outward bound on a cruise in 2004. *Author*

highest ratings of space per passenger among the larger modern cruise ships. And the established Cunard service standards characterise every aspect of their operation.

Inevitably, though, facing spiralling ship design and construction costs, Cunard was, for the first time, compelled to opt for what are, in a sense, 'off-the-peg' vessels for these, its most recent fleet additions, the two virtually-identical cruise sisters *Queen Victoria* and *Queen Elizabeth*. But even they have been customised to meet the peculiar needs of the Cunard operation which is focused on a clientele who appreciate the very British flavour that these ships convey. The decision to make the *Queen Elizabeth* slightly larger, with more cabin accommodation, is a reflection of the success that Cunard enjoys in this sector of the leisure industry.

Without doubt, each of Cunard's incomparable Queens has had a precise and definite raison d'etre, as the foregoing notes demonstrate. Complementing that, each Queen shares other distinctive attributes.

Each one, in the past and still today, exudes an onboard ambience steeped in elegance. Their trademark 'White Star' shipboard service helps make every passenger feel they are treated as someone special. It may be the glamour of dressing for dinner, of sipping a Martini in one of the stylish cocktail bars, or gliding around the dance floor of the Grand Lounge, maybe even taking in a show in a private box in a multi-tiered theatre or having afternoon tea, a particularly British tradition, served by white-gloved waiters. It is all of these facets and many more which together create that sense of refinement which is quintessentially the Queens' unique character. It is all part of what has made each of them, in its era, stand out from its contemporaries.

Of course, like no other passenger ships, the Queens also have a distinctive heritage and ancestry. Going back to the *Queen Mary*, the first of the Queen liners, while she was conceived as a Cunard ship she was to become the first-born of Cunard White Star parentage after those two great shipping institutions, probably the

sophisticated alternative – a style of cruising that mirrors the glamour of liner voyages of the past but in exotic locations. Yet the Cunard product remains affordable, permitting a discerning general public to enjoy an experience that was once the preserve of the rich and privileged.

Having already had undoubted success in this arena, Cunard was prompted to elevate its cruise experience in the form of larger ships, yet, as on the *QE2* in the past, the intimacy of the smaller cruise ship has been preserved on these new cruising Queens. They are not crowded. Indeed, with relatively modest passenger complements for their size, they have among the

two most famous shipping companies ever, were merged to ensure that the 'Big Ship' policy could come to fruition. For her and her five antecedents it is a lineage that, in genealogical terms, parallels the great monarchical dynasties of history. Moreover, they have inherited from both parent companies the proud traditions of quality and service that were established and perpetuated from their earliest origins in Victorian times.

Likewise, the Queens have a unique and special association with British royalty, both in the names they carry and in the patrons who bestowed those names upon them. It is a dimension that publicly defines them, setting them apart from the rest.

Cunard produced souvenir booklets to commemorate the entry into service of both the *Queen Mary* and the *Queen Elizabeth* – a 'Book of Comparisons' for the former and a 'Book of Facts' for the latter – each intended to convey the vast scale of these great ships. The quantities of materials used in their construction and the volumes of food commodities consumed on each voyage were conveyed in vivid descriptions using a range of superlatives, while their dimensions were highlighted in sketches that contrasted them with familiar buildings and landmarks. Exploiting the same broad theme and layout, a modern equivalent by Elspeth Wills (Open Agency) was published to coincide with the inauguration of the *Queen Mary 2*. Whereas each of those publications illustrated the grandeur and scale of those Queens by comparing them with other well-known, non-maritime structures, in this book the contrast is made, largely visually, between the Queens themselves.

Supported by a gallery of pictures, this book is an appreciation of each Queen in all its glory – the unmistakeable exterior forms and the sumptuous interiors. It also explores some of their behind-the-scenes inner workings and key functional features – how they are propelled and navigated, where the culinary delights for which they are renowned are prepared and delivered, how passenger comfort and safety are assured, how essential commodities such as water and

electricity are produced and managed, how the onboard entertainment has evolved, indeed how passengers' needs in many respects were and are so attentively and efficiently provided. By dissecting these floating palaces in a measure of detail to scrutinise their anatomy we will see, not only how the technology has evolved over the 75 or so years of their existence but also how, in each Queen, those standards of superlative performance have been achieved and sustained.

And that, in a nutshell, is the aim of this book.

*It should be noted that the grades of accommodation aboard the* Queen Mary *and* Queen Elizabeth *were known by different names before and after the Second World War. To avoid confusion when describing amenities on these ships, I have referred throughout to their classes as First, Second and Third, which is in effect what they were. The following table shows the relationship between these nominal identities and the actual names used and the periods in which each applied:*

| 1936-1945 | 1946-1968 | NOMINAL CLASS |
|---|---|---|
| Cabin | First | First |
| Tourist | Cabin | Second |
| Third | Tourist | Third |

*Abbreviations*

| | |
|---|---|
| cyl. | cylinders |
| DR | double reduction |
| FP | fixed pitch |
| mph | miles per hour |
| psi | pounds per square inch |
| SR | single reduction |
| VP | variable pitch |

The *Queen Mary* seen off Gilkicker Point, in the Solent, late in her career, illustrating how this wonderful liner retained her majesty to the last. The well in her foredeck, just ahead of her foremast, a feature that was unique to her among the first two Queens, may be clearly seen in this view. Her large white ventilators are also conspicuous.

*Barry Elliott*

# Cunard's Legendary Queens

DESIGNING THE *QUEEN MARY* confronted Cunard with as great a challenge as had the decision to implement its radical concept for the future transatlantic passenger service. Her construction and that of her forthcoming sister would involve a major commitment of Company funds, a massive, possibly crippling, investment and it was vital that everything had to be right to minimise the financial risks.

As Neil Potter and Jack Frost put it in their book *The Mary*: "With a ship of this character and type, a new venture in marine design, revolutionary in so many ways, and with her immense prestige value, with the eyes of the world watching every development, the Company realised it was presented with an [enormous] challenge".

Surveying the contemporary scene, it was evident that liner design was in a period of transition. The giant liners of the late Edwardian era looked decidedly dated. But should Cunard play safe and follow tradition or go for a more extreme, cutting edge look for these high-profile new ships? Early impressions reveal there was a measure of prevarication before a configuration was settled upon that fell, safely and sensibly, between ultra-modern and more conventionally progressive.

The differences between Cunard's Queens begin, in fact, at the most basic level, in the methods and materials of their construction. The *Queen Mary* was built, as were the *Queen Elizabeth* and later the *Queen Elizabeth 2*, according to the techniques that prevailed for much of the twentieth century.

Fabricated on an open slipway, exposed to the elements, and starting with the longitudinal keel section, from which a skeletal structure of ribs, frames and beams grew upwards, her hull gradually emerged as plating work progressed. The culmination was the launch of the completed hull to permit fitting-out to commence. Subsequent drydocking was an essential requisite of the process, to permit the removal of the residual launch paraphernalia still attached to her underwater hull. Fundamentally, her construction followed a time-consuming vertical direction in which key stages occurred sequentially.

In contrast, the three most recent Queens have been built from the outset in an enclosed and sheltered drydock, obviating the necessity to subject their hulls to the stresses of a conventional launch. For them, construction followed a horizontal rather than vertical direction whereby modular sections, prefabricated elsewhere in the shipyard and delivered to the assembly basin, were joined together one-by-one along the ship's length from the bow to the stern. When assembled, the largely finished ships – much of the fitting-out having taken place concurrently with fabrication of the hull – were simply floated by flooding the drydock.

The cost benefits of these modern construction techniques can be measured by comparing build durations, bearing in mind that time is money. While under construction a ship, especially an expensive Queen, is an investment giving no return.

The *Queen Mary 2* took 22 months to complete from the cutting of first steel in January 2002 to her sea trials in November 2003. The original *Queen Mary*, on the other hand, took some 36 months, 64 per cent longer, from the laying of her first keel plates through to readiness for delivery, even allowing for the period of idleness when all work was temporarily suspended at the height of the Great Depression. But, working shifts around the clock, the construction of the latest Queen, the *Queen Elizabeth*, took still less time, breaking all the records. Just 15 months elapsed from when her keel was laid in July 2009 to her delivery in October 2010, the fastest ever build of a passenger ship of her size and type.

**ABOVE** Following her post-War refit, the *Queen Elizabeth* is seen on speed trials in the Firth of Clyde on 8 October 1946, prior to making her first commercial voyage. A contemporary verse by Sir Alan Herbert attested to her transition from wartime auxiliary to peacetime flagship, part of which reads: "At last young giant, infant of the fleet, your medals on, you sail down civvy street. Here come your passengers but who will check, the ghosts of soldiers crowding on your deck?" *Cunard Archives – University of Liverpool*

As ships of exquisite complexity and splendour, the Queens have not been cheap to build but savings in the shipyard have been critical to the viability of the latest ships of this class.

Generally speaking, while steel has remained the principal construction material, the method of assembly has also changed dramatically, with significant benefits. On the *Queen Mary* and *Queen Elizabeth*, the hull plates were attached to the ribs and beams using tens of millions of rivets, red hot steel pins hammered flush on either side so that, as they cooled and contracted, the plates – caulked for water-tightness – were secured tightly.

Viewed close up, the *Queen Mary*'s mighty structure, peppered with rivets, gave the impression of enormous

strength that could withstand anything that the elements or the oceans might throw at her. By the time the *Queen Elizabeth 2* had been ordered, riveted construction had become largely obsolete and her hull and superstructure, like that of the later *Queen Mary 2* and the cruise ships *Queen Victoria* and *Queen Elizabeth*, was welded.

Without wishing to state the obvious, the process of rod welding involves joining butted plates together along their seams using electrodes. A filler, added between the locally melted plate edges, forms a pool of molten material (the weld pool) that cools to become an immensely strong joint. In effect, the adjoining plates become one.

Besides giving their hulls a smoother finish, reducing underwater resistance and, as a consequence, fuel consumption, the absence of rivets also represents a considerable decrease in weight, a matter that also influences fuel economics. The rivets used in the construction of the *Queen Mary* weighed 4,000 tons or 8 per cent of the 50,000 tons weight of her hull and machinery. Pushing less weight around the oceans relative to gross tonnage constitutes another valuable fuel-saving measure.

By comparing the figures for displacement tonnage (weight of displaced water) and gross tonnage (internal volumetric capacity) of each of the Queens, as shown in the Vital Statistics tables on pages 89-93, it can be seen that the *Queen Mary* and first *Queen Elizabeth* weighed virtually the same as the *Queen Mary 2*, a ship of almost twice their size in gross tonnage terms. To some extent their high fuel consumption reflected this disparity.

As it turned out, fate determined that the *Queen Mary* would be the second rather than the first ocean liner to exceed 1,000 ft (305 metres) in length, although she was the first to top 80,000 gross registered tons. Inevitably, during the early years of her career, she was measured in all respects against the contemporary *Normandie* of the French Line whose début was a year earlier. Externally, hers was an evolved design, a progression from the 20-year old *Aquitania*, Cunard's previous newly-built express

ABOVE The *Queen Mary* was a "rampart of a ship" as John Masefield described her in his poem "Number 534" and as conveyed graphically in this observation of her lofty superstructure. *World Ship Society/Austen Harrison*

RIGHT This aerial view of the *Queen Elizabeth* shows her bow anchor and flush foredeck. The *QE2* was the only other Queen to have three forward anchors, although the bow anchor was later removed. The fiddley casings with their grills, used for engine room ventilation, are the white-painted structures immediately beneath each funnel. *Cunard Archives – University of Liverpool*

liner, whereas that of her Gallic competitor was more radical in appearance, exhibiting a flair that corresponded to her extraordinary interiors.

Comparing them visually, the *Queen Mary* was as much British in her character – robust, powerful, sturdy and workmanlike – as the chic, enigmatic *Normandie* was French. Typifying the apparent national differences between the *Queen Mary* and *Normandie* was their foghorns. The *Queen Mary* had steam whistles that emitted a deep, rich tone keyed to lower bass 'A', a sound which made you tingle. It was a throaty bellow compared to the fluty, triple-tone siren of the *Normandie*. The *Queen Elizabeth* was

LEFT The *Queen Mary*'s foredeck, cluttered with the gear for mooring, anchor handling and the stowage and discharge of cargo, looked extremely busy when contrasted with that of her French rival, the *Normandie*, or the later QE2. *Andrew Kilk*

RIGHT In contrast, the *Queen Elizabeth 2*'s forecastle, viewed from below her bridge, is strikingly clear. The breakwater, designed to help keep water off her foredeck, can be seen just ahead of the rows of inflatable life-rafts. *Author*

RIGHT Sailing from Southampton, a striking view of the graceful lines of the *Queen Elizabeth*. She was described as "the last of a great age" and as "engineering and aesthetics finally brought together". *Mick Lindsay*

fitted likewise. So impressive was her distinctive call that it was once described as "a roar of freedom from her mighty voice".

The *Queen Mary* was not intended to look too modern but, though she may have been slightly behind the times, with decks that were rather cluttered compared to the *Normandie*'s unhampered open spaces, she triumphed where it counted most: on the bottom line. Critically, with her accommodation distributed by class along more traditional lines, the *Queen Mary* made an operating profit, without Government financial assistance, over the four seasons from 1936 to 1939 while her French rival clocked up heavily-subsidised losses.

The *Queen Mary* was only the second Cunard passenger ship to have a rounded cruiser stern, a modern feature compared with the *Aquitania*'s overhanging counter, while her bow was raked rather than straight. Other distinguishing features were her three huge red and black funnels supported by external wire guys and the four, square section grilled engine-room ventilators on either side of her Sports Deck. She had a forward well-deck, a feature not repeated in her later, flush-decked half-sister *Queen Elizabeth*.

Whether it was the fact that her maiden voyage, planned to coincide with Cunard's 100th anniversary, had to be aborted because of the outbreak of war or because the *Queen Mary* had already won the heart of the nation, not least as a symbol of recovery from the Great Depression, but the *Queen Elizabeth* was always to some extent in the shadow of her older consort. Referred to as "the forgotten Queen", she had less of a following and was in a way the unsung partner of the famous double act.

In reality, though, the *Queen Elizabeth* was a beautiful, graceful ocean liner of legendary elegance and splendour whose design was a refinement of that of the *Queen Mary*. She was the sleeker of the two with cleaner lines externally, the result of engineering-led design improvements. Fewer, more powerful boilers, apart from freeing up inside space for larger public areas, meant that only two, broader funnel uptakes were required to exhaust boiler smoke, which gave her a more balanced profile and they were supported internally, eliminating many of the guys that had surrounded the *Mary*'s funnels. Also, as she had grilled fiddley casings to provide engine room ventilation (partially raised decks around the funnels, over the engine and boiler rooms, to let the hot air and fumes from the working areas escape), the *Queen Elizabeth* had no need for the many large cowls that detrimentally dominated the *Queen Mary*'s appearance.

The incorporation of a third, bower anchor required her to have a more sharply raked stem to ensure that it would fall clear of her hull when released, making her the longer of the pair by twelve feet. Despite these differences, the *Queen Elizabeth* was in many respects more or less a repeat of the *Queen Mary*.

As conceived and as delivered, the *Queen Elizabeth 2* was a complete departure from the style and construction of the earlier Queens. Though her erratic, uncertain genesis no doubt had a bearing on this, it was also determined in part by her very different purpose as well as the impact of the artistic and design influences of the era in which she was commissioned; the Swinging Sixties – a period of great change socially, economically and in shipping practice.

Looking at her structural composition in more detail, it can be seen that the *QE2* represented a significant milestone in liner

ABOVE The *Queen Elizabeth 2* enters the water for the first time on 20 September 1967, the last Cunard Queen to be launched in traditional fashion. HM Queen Elizabeth II, her patron, has been present at the launches or naming ceremonies of all three *Queen Elizabeth*'s plus the *Queen Mary 2*. Compare this picture with the one on page 26. *Cunard*

design development. Aluminium was used extensively in her five uppermost decks and her superstructure was distinctive for its rounded corners and moulded shapes. Smooth-sided and enclosed for full air-conditioning, she looked streamlined.

The *Queen Elizabeth 2* was the first Cunard Queen aboard which cargo stowage and associated handling equipment was almost completely dispensed with. The containerisation revolution was in full swing by the late 1960s and the vast majority of freight traffic had already been diverted to specialised vessels. Besides which, the *QE2* was first and foremost a pure passenger ship. Her unique dual role was not consistent with the conveyance of cargo. Thus, her foredeck, concealed within a graceful sheer that blended into the forward end of her superstructure, was much clearer compared with

ABOVE Looking at the *Queen Elizabeth* close-up while she was berthed alongside Southampton's first Ocean Terminal, her side plating reveals some of the millions of rivets that characterised the external appearance of the first two Queens. *World Ship Society/ Austen Harrison*

RIGHT A close-up view of the *Queen Victoria* shows the smoother hull finish that resulted from welded construction, with just a patchwork of weld seams. *The Queen Elizabeth 2, Queen Mary 2 and new Queen Elizabeth also have welded hulls. Author*

**RIGHT** The *Queen Elizabeth 2* when she first entered service, sporting her original, controversially shaped and coloured funnel. In contrast, her graceful curved and raked bow drew nothing but praise. Note how, compared with later photographs, there is a total absence of any satellite navigation radomes on her upper deck. *Cunard*

She also has a partial turtle-back like the French super-liner to keep water off her foredeck.

The *Queen Victoria* and new *Queen Elizabeth*, both derived from the Fincantieri 'Vista' class, having benefited from significant redesign, have hulls and upper structures that have been lengthened by the insertion of an additional 9 metre (29.5 feet) section. This, along with other refinements and internal restyling, has made them essentially a distinct sub-class, exclusive to Cunard.

The *QE2*'s singular flaw was, in the opinion of many, her original funnel, its form apparently contrived through extensive wind tunnel tests. The proud crimson and black funnels of the original Queens were their principal identifying feature, a kind of emblematic trademark. In the revolutionary *Queen Elizabeth 2*, the apparent abandonment of this well-known and vital visual manifestation caused quite a furore. The space-age shape of the funnel was one thing but, the greater heresy, it wasn't even painted in Cunard's traditional colours. Already the subject of much negative criticism from the purists, no other aspect of the new ship's design was greeted with greater disdain. When, later, her funnel was painted Cunard red and black and, later still, when it was replaced by a more substantial 'true flue', the changes were welcomed by Cunard devotees.

The enhancements introduced in the design of the *Queen Elizabeth 2* have been taken further in the most recent Queens. Novel enhancements to hull shape, permitted by their evolved functions, have been adopted to improve both economic performance and sea-kindliness.

For example, the bulbous extension at the base of the *QE2*'s rounded stem, itself a profound departure from the knife-like bows of her predecessors, protrudes significantly further forward on the *Queen Mary 2*, *Queen Victoria* and *Queen Elizabeth*. Where the *Queen Mary* and *Queen Elizabeth* had a straight rake at the bow, the *QE2* sported an elegantly curved and raked stem profile, a style that has been enhanced on the *Queen Mary 2* to

her predecessors. Gone were the tall, pencil masts with their derricks along with much of the heavy winch gear the old Queens had required. In their place, she exhibited a graceful open deck space with rounded breakwater and, though her anchor chains remained on her foredeck, the machinery used for docking and mooring along with other equipment was largely concealed from view.

Compared to the earlier Queens, the modern trio, particularly the *Queen Victoria* and new *Queen Elizabeth*, have much shorter foredecks, a characteristic of pure cruise ships. On this pair the bridge height is about the same as its distance from the forepeak. Notably, on the foredeck of the *Queen Mary 2*, the breakwater barrier has been augmented, its profile V-shaped akin to that of the *Normandie* rather than curved.

create a distinctive radically-finer, clipper-like shape that suits being driven hard through rough seas. The *Queen Victoria* and new *Queen Elizabeth*, in contrast, have a gentle convex curve to their flared and raked bows, emphasised by a painted sheer.

Stern shapes are another design feature that have been modified in keeping with the prevailing wisdom of modern naval architectural thinking. Both the *Queen Victoria* and *Queen Elizabeth* have transom or squared type sterns, in either case angled inward down to the level of Deck 1, a style commonly employed on modern cruise ships. But what of the *Queen Mary 2*? Whereas the transom stern is considered to be better hydrodynamically, aiding propulsive efficiency, the spoon stern of the *QE2* and the cruiser sterns of the older *Queen Mary* and *Queen Elizabeth* were the preferred choice for sea-keeping, particularly when pitching was experienced. Stephen Payne's solution for the cruise liner *Queen Mary 2*, the Queen that, besides cruising, would be continuing with transatlantic voyages in all weathers, was to combine these stern types together by adopting what is known as a modified Costanzi stern.

By the time that the *Queen Mary 2* emerged, acceptance of progressive ship design had reached the point where she had an almost traditional look. Of course much of what makes her unique, apart from her size, is hidden inside her, designed integrally within her structure. To ensure her capability of operating in the harshest sea conditions without compromising speed, she was required to have greater structural strength than the *Queen Elizabeth 2*, the Queen that she was in a sense replacing. Unlike the *QE2*, which has a high percentage of aluminium in her superstructure, the *Queen Mary 2* is built entirely of steel.

Like the *Queen Mary 2*, the equally robust construction of the *Queen Mary* and *Queen Elizabeth*, specified to permit operation in all seasons on the broad expanse of the Atlantic, known for its ferocious storms, proved valuable for another, unexpected diversion – the punishing demands of troopship service during the Second World War.

At a time when regular overhauls and dock maintenance became rare events, certainly occurring a lot less frequently than would have been the case in peacetime, the *Queen Mary* and *Queen Elizabeth* clocked up extraordinary mileages carrying record complements to and from all theatres of combat. Hulls and engines took a pounding, their durability a testament to the quality of workmanship that had gone into them.

While the later *Queen Elizabeth 2* was called upon to perform a single troop-carrying voyage, at the time of the Falklands Conflict in 1982, there is not even the remotest likelihood that any of Cunard's current trio of Queens will ever be requisitioned to perform such duties.

ABOVE *The Queen Elizabeth 2* seen at Southampton's Queen Elizabeth II terminal on 7 June 2003, some 18 years after her engine refit and other, subsequent modifications which created additional penthouse suites. This was her ultimate external appearance. Her upper decks now carry an array of satellite radomes and other telecommunications devices. *Author*

ABOVE The *Queen Mary 2* sails from New York, leaving Manhattan Island behind. Her funnel height was modified to allow a minimum clearance under the Verrazano Narrows Bridge, connecting Brooklyn with Staten Island, of just 10 feet at high tide. *Cunard*

ABOVE The *Queen Mary* approaches New York at the end of a transatlantic voyage. Compare this picture with that of the *Queen Mary 2* [*left*] and notice how there is little difference between the skyscraper background of Manhattan Island in the two pictures. This view was taken before the World Trade Center was constructed while the former was taken after the destruction of the twin towers on 11 September 2001. *Cunard*

Wartime roles not only exposed the Queens to abnormal wear and tear but also to the constant risk of enemy attack. Where the *Queen Mary* and *Queen Elizabeth* relied on their high speed to evade German U-boats, operating independently of convoys, this was of little value to the QE2 which faced very different hazards during her brief diversion to auxiliary duties. Had the Argentines been able to sink her, either by air force jets or Exocet missiles, they would have scored a huge psychological victory and the threat posed by those weapons was not an easy one to counter. Hence, the QE2 performed only a single out and back trooping run and, for the duration of her time in the war zone, she was kept as far out of harm's way as possible, in the proximity of the relatively greater shelter of South Georgia.

Hull strength and integrity have had yet another benefit for the Queens, in the form of longevity. The *Queen Mary* survived in operation for a commendable 31 years after her entry into service (33 years from when she was launched). The *Queen Elizabeth*'s active life lasted a comparable length of time, although her sea-going career was ended prematurely on 9 January 1972 when she was destroyed by fire at Hong Kong while undergoing conversion to become the cruising campus *Seawise University*. She was then 32 years old.

Thanks to a series of life-extending refits, including a major engine conversion begun in her 18th season, the *Queen Elizabeth 2* outlasted both her predecessors to become the

**LEFT** The abundance of open space on the *Queen Mary 2*'s upper decks can be appreciated in this view taken in mid-Atlantic. *Author*

**ABOVE** Compare the previous picture with this photograph of the *Queen Mary*'s cluttered Sports Deck dominated by large square ventilators, here seen stretching along her portside in this view taken at Long Beach. *Andrew Kilk*

**FAR LEFT** The *Queen Mary 2* outward bound in the Solent showing her unusual Costanzi-type stern. *Author*

**LEFT** Taken from almost the same position, this is the transom-type stern of the later *Queen Victoria*. *Author*

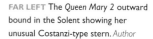

ABOVE The tiered balconies of the *Queen Elizabeth*'s outside cabins and suites, a characteristic design feature that is equally a dimension of the larger *Queen Mary 2*, reflecting the cruise ship influence on the style of their upperworks. *Author*

longest-serving Cunard ship ever, at 42 years from when she was launched. Still afloat and capable of more sea time, the career of this popular Cunarder only came to an end because of the unjustifiably high costs that would have been involved to bring her up to the standard of the latest and most stringent SOLAS (Safety of Life at Sea) passenger ship safety regulations.

Concern about the durability of the aluminium in her superstructure, though justified, proved to be overstated. Perhaps the most incredible aspect of her record longevity is that the *Queen Elizabeth 2* still looked strikingly modern when she finally left the Cunard fleet in November 2008.

The *Queen Elizabeth 2*'s long life span may seem, on the face of it, to have been extraordinary, but endurability of this calibre is now expected routinely of the *Queen Mary 2*, *Queen Victoria* and *Queen Elizabeth*. Life expectancy of up to forty years has been designed and built into their structures.

ABOVE During sea trials, the new *Queen Elizabeth* was deliberately heeled over to 35 degrees, her engines were run at 100 per cent power and she was put through speed turns. All essential tests were passed without a hitch. Her delivery voyage was also a test in itself of her engines and systems. Here she is seen arriving at Southampton for the first time on 8 October 2010. Her modified stern arrangement, the result of extending the accommodation structure aft-wards above Deck 5, is the principal distinguishing feature between her and the *Queen Victoria*, accounting for an increase of her tonnage measurement of almost 900 gross tons. *Cunard*

RIGHT The *Queen Elizabeth* sails from Southampton's new Ocean Terminal on 12 October 2010 at the start of her maiden voyage. As an indication of the popularity of cruising Cunard style, tickets for her maiden cruise were sold out within 30 minutes of becoming available. *Cunard*

The *Queen Victoria* in drydock at Marghera, Italy, on the occasion of her official floating out on 15 January 2007. She became buoyant for the first time with the flooding of the graving dock. The traditional naming ceremony took place eleven months later, following her delivery. With her underwater hull still exposed to view, her pronounced bulbous bow can be seen, as well as the three openings to her side thrusters which have metal grills to prevent objects reaching and damaging the thruster blades. *Fincantieri*

# The Power and The Glory

IN THE LATE 1920s, as the conception of what was to become the *Queen Mary* gradually emerged in all its details in draughtsmen's blueprints, the economical diesel or internal combustion engine was in the ascendancy. Barely two decades later, some 90 per cent or more of new mercantile vessels would have this type of engine installed. Yet the marine steam engine, effectively the steam turbine, remained the preferred choice where high speed was a principal requirement. Cunard's four-and-a-half-day Atlantic express service was such a case in point.

Besides their capability of producing greater power output to drive the propellers, steam turbines also benefited from lower maintenance costs as well as from causing less noise and vibration, matters of real concern to those passengers whose accommodation was located closest to the engine spaces. Captain James Bissett once bestowed fitting praise on the *Queen Mary* when he said, "She performed beautifully, just like a sewing machine".

Steam engines are also known for their reliability. The fact that the *Queen Elizabeth* put to sea in 1940 without any sea trials and few engineering checks, yet ran perfectly, was a great tribute to both her turbines and boilers and the quality of workmanship that had gone into them. On the downside, though, the boilers of steamships had to be kept fired up at all times while in operational service, a costly drain on fuel during long port turnrounds.

Both the *Queen Mary* and the *Queen Elizabeth* had Parsons steam turbines, constructed under licence by their builders, John Brown at Clydebank. The *Queen Elizabeth 2* was also a steam-turbine-powered ship up until her engine conversion in 1986. In her case the turbines were built to the designs of Pametrada, into which the Parsons company name had transmogrified. The turbine sets comprised High Pressure (HP), Intermediate Pressure (IP) and Low Pressure (LP) ahead turbines with astern blading in the IP and LP casings.

Fundamental to the operation of steam turbine machinery is high pressure steam, delivered to the turbine chambers from boilers located further forward along the hull. In simple terms, the layout followed the longitudinal sequence: boilers, turbines, gearing, propeller shafts and screw propellers, with key components separated into different watertight compartments.

The *Queen Mary* was fitted out with the latest marine boilers of the Yarrow water-tube variety, twenty-four in all for the main engines, whose thermal efficiency was second to none. Oil fired, they could deliver steam superheated to 700 degrees F (Fahrenheit) and 400 psi (pounds per square inch) pressure.

The selection of water-tube boilers for the *Queen Mary* was one that aroused considerable debate, not least because preliminary designs had been based on the use of Scotch boilers, a heavier but tried and proven alternative. The replacement choice raised issues of stability as they would affect the ship's metacentric height, problems that were overcome by a certain amount of redesign.

Subsequent improvements to boiler design permitted the number required on the *Queen Elizabeth* to be reduced to twelve and on the *Queen Elizabeth 2* to just three. In either case, the steam conditions were enhanced to 425 psi at 750 degrees F and 850 psi at 1,000 degrees F respectively.

Normal practice, because the turbines rotated faster than the propeller shafts, was to employ intermediate reduction gearing to manage the rotational speed. In the case of the *Queen Mary* and *Queen Elizabeth* it was single reduction (SR) gearing whereas, thirty years later, the selection of higher speed turbines for the

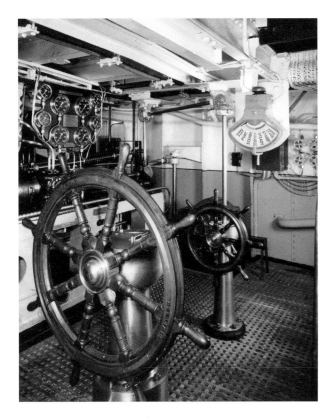

FAR LEFT The steering gear machinery controls of the *Queen Mary*, a heavy and complex electro-hydraulic system that converted helm instructions from the bridge into movements of the ship's huge rudder. *Cunard Archives – University of Liverpool*

LEFT The two starboard-side propellers and the immense 140-ton hinged rudder of the *Queen Elizabeth* exposed to view while she was still on the stocks prior to her launch. The tips of the propeller blades are temporarily protected from damage by sections of rubber car tyres. *Cunard Archives – University of Liverpool*

RIGHT One of the *Queen Mary*'s four propeller shafts that extended some 250 or more feet along her underwater hull. The nearest collar is a torsionmeter, used to measure the horsepower of the shaft. *Cunard Archives – University of Liverpool*

*Queen Elizabeth 2* necessitated double reduction (DR) gearing to convert the rotational power to her twin propeller shafts. Astern movement was achieved by shutting off the main manoeuvring valves and carefully opening the astern valves, a delicate operation if torsional stresses in the turbine rotors were to be avoided.

The selection of this engine configuration for these prestigious liners was all about achieving the speed that their regular weekly Atlantic schedules demanded. It was also, to some extent, about record-breaking, certainly in the early years when the *Queen Mary* vied with the *Normandie* for Blue Riband honours. The

*Normandie* may have had flair compared to her British counterpart but, as it was to prove, style certainly wasn't everything for one of the defining factors was speed. And though the margin between them wasn't huge, the *Queen Mary* was always the faster of the two. Having established record crossing times in both directions, she went on to hold the Atlantic Blue Riband for 14 years.

Although the *Queen Elizabeth* never held the speed record for the Atlantic crossing, she was the fastest of the pair having achieved a maximum speed on trials that was around 3.5 knots (4 mph) faster than the *Queen Mary*'s best time. Cunard presumably

**FUEL CONSUMPTION, STORAGE CAPACITY AND DURATION**

| | Engines | Propulsion | Fuel Capacity | Daily Fuel Consumption | Duration |
|---|---|---|---|---|---|
| **Queen Mary** | 4 x 4 steam turbines 24 boilers | Quadruple screw | 8,630 tons | 1,075 tons | 8 days |
| **Queen Elizabeth** | 4 x 4 steam turbines 12 boilers | Quadruple screw | ca. 8,400 tons | 1,050 tons | 8 days |
| **Queen Elizabeth 2** *(as a steamship)* | 4 steam turbines 3 boilers | Twin screw | 6,517 tons | 520 tons | 12 days |
| **Queen Elizabeth 2** *(as a diesel ship)* | Diesel Generators | Twin screw | 4,715 tons | 380 tons | 12 days |
| **Queen Mary 2** | Combined Diesel & Gas Turbine Generators (CODAG) | Quadruple pod | 8,291 tonnes | 498 tonnes | 17 days |
| **Queen Victoria & Queen Elizabeth** | Diesel Generators | Twin pod | 3,185 tonnes | 263 tonnes | 12 days |

NB. Consumption and duration are at the same service speed of 28.5 knots (32.8 mph) except for the *Queen Victoria* and *Queen Elizabeth* where they are calculated at the cruising speed of 22.5 knots

For approximate conversion 1 metric tonne = 287 US gallons = 1.085 m³ and 1 metric tonne = 0.9842 UK (long) tons or 1.1023 US (short) tons

considered it unnecessary to put her fully through her paces when there were no other competitors on the immediate post-war Atlantic scene capable of wresting the Atlantic Blue Riband from the *Queen Mary*. When the *United States* entered the Atlantic service in 1952, her margin of speed superiority was so great that it rendered a challenge by the *Queen Elizabeth* as completely pointless.

What the Queens lost in terms of speed superiority was more than compensated for by their joint operation, enabling regular weekly sailings to be made from Southampton and New York. Yet, despite the fact that they were no longer the fastest ships on the Atlantic run, they remained capable of maintaining an express service and, when called upon, they could respond to the throttle. A contemporary description said of them that they were "grand ladies that could lift up their skirts to make a dash when they needed to".

A major disadvantage of the steam turbine power plant, because of its many bulky components, was its weight and space demand within the hull. Later on, from the mid-1950s onwards following the Suez crisis, the cost of fuel also became a critical factor in the operating economics of the Queens, constituting the difference between a profit- or loss-making operation. As

### STAFF TRANSITION FROM TECHNICAL TO HOTEL & CATERING DEPARTMENTS

| | Technical Staff | | Hotel & Catering Staff | |
|---|---|---|---|---|
| | Number | Percentage of total staff | Number | Percentage of total staff |
| **Queen Mary** | 254 | 20 | 829 | 65 |
| **Queen Elizabeth 2** | 93 | 9 | 860 | 85 |
| **Queen Mary 2** | 99 | 9 | 976 | 85 |

Hotel Department includes all Pursers, Stewards and persons engaged in passenger care other than food service

Catering Department includes all restaurant, kitchen and bar staff

Technical Department includes, besides engine-room staff, all persons engaged in the mechanical and maintenance operations except carpentry

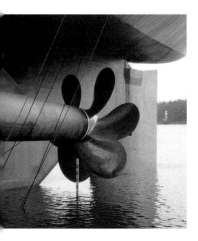

**ABOVE** Compared to the four-bladed propellers of the *Queen Mary* and *Queen Elizabeth*, those of the *Queen Elizabeth 2*, when she first entered service, were specially designed six-bladed fixed-pitch propellers. *Cunard*

their express service was sold on its regularity and faster crossing time, savings could not be made by simply reducing speed. Already passenger numbers were falling as airliners increasingly eroded the more lucrative end of the market, itself auguring the imminent end of the scheduled ocean passage option and, with it, the demise of Cunard's first two Queens.

The matter of fuel consumption, now more than ever, is a vital one insofar as the economics of ship operation are concerned. It is a widely held view that shipping lines or cruise operators have three main costs to bear: labour costs, fuel costs and vessel acquisition costs, the latter generally amortised over a projected lifespan for new vessels. Although these days crew members are often engaged from low-wage countries for employment in certain onboard departments, there are nevertheless limits to what can be accomplished without running the risk of compromising quality of service, another important ingredient of the Cunard product. Fuel costs, therefore, offer the next greatest potential for savings in the drive for operational economies.

Mention has been made of specific advances in marine engineering technology whereby boiler numbers were reduced as their thermal efficiency improved and this had tangible benefits in terms of both reduced engine room manning levels and lower fuel consumption. The latter can be best illustrated by the table detailing the fuel consumption, storage capacity and duration of three generations of Queens (*see page 29*).

On the *Queen Elizabeth 2*, a high degree of automation also contributed to reductions in engineering crew levels. As far as the impact of engineering improvements on staff strength are concerned, it should be remembered that where total crew numbers remain much the same, any Technical Department reductions translate directly into increases in the Hotel, Catering and Entertainment departments, those attending directly to passenger needs, areas in which Cunard has enjoyed conspicuous success.

In order to give the *Queen Elizabeth 2* a greater life expectancy or, put another way, a viable future, it became necessary to replace her costly, gas-guzzling turbines with diesel-electric machinery. The new engines comprised nine MAN/BMW 4-stroke, resiliently-mounted, medium speed diesels supplying power to two GEC (MW) AC electric motors, each of which was directly coupled to a single propeller shaft. With the diesels running at 400 revs/min, the electrical generators were each capable of producing a total of 10.5 megawatts at 10,000 volts. The new configuration was lighter and occupied less space. More importantly it resulted in even greater fuel savings. At 380 tons per day, consumption was barely over a third of what the *Queen Mary* had burnt, even though a broadly similar number of passengers were being carried at the same service speed. Indeed, diesel technology had developed to such a degree that it would now be associated with high speed as well as economic operation and, to prove the point, on post-modification acceptance trials the *Queen Elizabeth 2* achieved the amazing top speed of 34.1 knots (39.3 mph). This was almost two knots better than the maximum speed achieved on her original builder's trials in 1969.

Given such improvements in performance, it may come as a surprise to realise that marine power and propulsion technology have taken yet another quantum leap forward since the inception of the *Queen Elizabeth 2*, even since the time when she was re-engined. In the types of prime mover, the ratios of engine power to weight, and in the methods by which engine power is converted into propulsive power, there is now very little similarity with the past. And, probably the greatest gain from this engineering revolution has been the release of hull space hitherto demanded for the location of engine plant and auxiliary equipment at the expense of accommodation and recreational space. Besides that, designers have gained the freedom to configure engine layout in ways that ensure the most beneficial allocation of hull space for the ship's primary purposes: passenger comfort, leisure and entertainment.

This brings us to the *Queen Mary 2* of 2004, one of the boldest and most innovative experiments in modern passenger ship engineering of the past half century. Dispensing with conventional screws, propeller shafts and rudder, she has electrically-driven podded propulsion units, which free up a vast amount of internal space, while her main CODAG (combined diesel and gas turbine) powerplant is a departure from every form of machinery previously fitted into the hull of a Cunard ship.

Her twin functions, making North Atlantic liner crossings in five to six days on the one hand and extended luxury cruises, on the other, required a configuration that could deliver both high speed and an economic cruising performance. Consequently, supplying electricity to the reversible motors of her four propulsion pods she has four Wartsila diesel-generators running on heavy fuel oil (HFO) and two General Electric gas turbine generators running on marine gas oil (MGO) to provide boost power whenever needed. The diesel and gas turbine units can be operated in any combination depending on service requirements, but wherever possible the greatest dependence is placed on the diesel generators because the fuel used by the gas turbines is much more expensive and, over an equivalent period, they consume a great deal more. Total daily fuel consumption at a service speed of 28.5 knots (32.8 mph) is 498 tonnes (261 tonnes

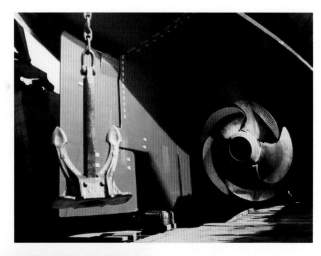

RIGHT After her conversion to diesel-electric power, the *Queen Elizabeth 2* was fitted with new four-bladed, variable-pitch screw propellers. From that point she no longer required reversing machinery. Her stern anchor hangs down in this drydock view. *Cunard*

LEFT The engine and propulsion systems of the current generation of Queen passenger ships are radically different to those of their predecessors. The adoption of the external propulsion pod with its own integral electric motor has permitted the elimination of gearing, propeller shafts, rudders and steering gear machinery. The *Queen Mary 2*'s entire engine installation is the largest marine power plant ever installed on a merchant ship. Note the skeg-type keel extension between the pods. *Alstom Chantiers de L'Atlantique*

of HFO and 237 tonnes of MGO), rather more than the *Queen Elizabeth 2*. However, despite this slight disadvantage, the engine arrangement of the *Queen Mary 2* provides greater operational flexibility and is more compact. An all diesel configuration to deliver a comparable total power output would have been bulky, requiring larger exhaust uptakes and water ducts which, in turn would have impacted on outside deck space and the available space for public rooms.

Contrasting the *Queen Mary 2* with the *Queen Mary*, it can be seen that, through the utilisation of external pods with their own integral electric drive motors, two fixed and two capable of rotating through 360 degrees (known as azimuth pods or 'Azipods' for short), dramatic changes have been made both in the appearance of the ship's underwater form when viewed in elevation and in the schematic distribution of the main engine machinery throughout the hull (*see opposite*). Gone are the long propeller shafts and traditional, drag-causing rudder. Equally, there is no longer a requirement for astern turbines, as provided on the *Queen Mary* and *Queen Elizabeth*, or of variable pitch propellers, as fitted to the re-engined *Queen Elizabeth 2*, for astern manoeuvring. Steering on the *Queen Mary 2*, including in reverse direction, is obtained using the reversible puller propellers of the rotating Rolls-Royce Mermaid 'Azipods'.

The net result is a huge reduction in the total amount of machinery required to drive the ship but, equally important, naval architect Stephen Payne was not, as a consequence, constrained in the way his earlier counterparts had been when laying out the constituent parts within the hull. Cable runs from the gas-turbine and diesel alternators and trunking for the diesel

LEFT Seen while she was drydocked at Southampton for overhaul, the bow thrusters of the *Queen Elizabeth 2* have pivoting butterfly valves as a means of minimising water resistance. The *Queen Mary 2* also has this arrangement. In her case the valves are chamfered for the smoothest fit into the tunnel apertures. *Wool–Hulton Archive-Getty Images*

engine exhausts have been laid along the most convenient routes with fewer inhibitions to the placement, dimensions and overall size of the public rooms.

In the *Queen Mary 2*, her main diesel plant is located low down in the hull, more or less in the position where the turbine engines would have been on the *Queen Mary*, *Queen Elizabeth* and *Queen Elizabeth 2* but her gas turbine units are positioned high up on Deck 13, in an enclosure immediately behind her funnel. This arrangement, which distributes weight within the hull to give the most ideal motion characteristics, as demonstrated and confirmed by countless tank tests with models, improves passenger comfort enormously. Also, the fact that the moving parts of the propulsion system are located outside the hull means that their vibration and noise have been virtually eliminated altogether.

Thus, the migration of engine technology since the 1930s has seen the horizontal engine layout of the *Queen Mary* give way to a more vertical configuration on the *Queen Mary 2*.

Though less complex than that of the *Queen Mary 2*, the diesel-electric engine arrangement of the cruise ships *Queen Victoria* and *Queen Elizabeth* follows a broadly similar configuration in that it comprises diesel generators supplying electrical power to drive the reversible motors of twin 'Azipods'. The diesels aboard the *Queen Victoria* are Wartsila-built Sulzer Vee-type medium speed units, four with 16 cylinders and two with 12 cylinders. On the *Queen Elizabeth*, American-built MaK (part of the Caterpillar Group) diesels have been selected, four of Vee-type with 12 cylinders and two Inline-type with 8 cylinders.

Mention should be made here of the ancillary drive facilities that have become a feature of Cunard's Queens beginning with the *Queen Elizabeth 2*. Bow and side thrusters have been incorporated into the underwater hulls of the *Queen Elizabeth 2* (four Denny Brown – two independent each side), the *Queen Mary 2* (three transverse Rolls-Royce with variable pitch propellers) and the *Queen Victoria* and *Queen Elizabeth* (three transverse Stone Kamewa with variable pitch propellers). It should be

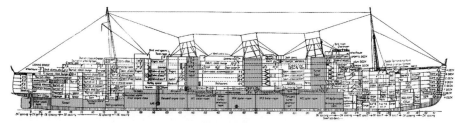

*Queen Mary*

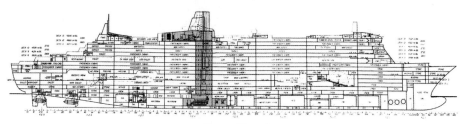

*Queen Mary 2*

remembered that early thrusters were less powerful than their modern equivalents. Also, they were activated by telegraph, requiring allowance to be made for the delay before their response could be felt. Today, controlled from the bridge, they give a degree of manoeuvrability at low speed that is so good the ships can be turned in just over their own length. Having the means to move them in this way has meant that the most recent Queens have enjoyed a much lower level of dependence on expensive ship-handling tugs when berthing or sailing. Typically, the old *Queen Mary* and *Queen Elizabeth* would have required the services of anything up to eight tugs, but on more than one occasion, notably at times when ports were hit by tug strikes, the *Queen Elizabeth 2* and *Queen Mary 2* have quickly and safely docked unaided. For the *Queen Victoria* and new *Queen Elizabeth* this is now routine practice when calling at Southampton's modern Ocean Terminal, with no more than two tugs standing by, rather than connected and rendering assistance.

ABOVE The amount of hull space consumed by the main machinery installation has reduced dramatically as these side elevations of the *Queen Mary* and *Queen Mary 2* clearly reveal.

The cross-looped RDF aerial of the *Queen Mary* may be seen at the front of her bridge with, behind it, her final radar scanner, in this photograph of her forward superstructure. *Shawn Drake*

# Passage of a Queen

THE BRIDGE OF THE MODERN QUEEN is a technological wonder and it is hard to believe that little more than three-quarters of a century ago on the *Queen Mary*, safe ahead navigation still, to a large extent, relied on the sharp sightedness of the Mk. 1 eyeball of the man on lookout in the crow's nest atop the foremast – a throwback to the days of the *Titanic* and earlier. A slight exaggeration, perhaps, but an indication of the progress made with electronic navigation systems since that time.

When she first entered service, the *Queen Mary* was equipped with the best and most advanced contemporary navigational equipment. Among it was a High Frequency (HF) Radio Direction Finding (RDF) receiver with its distinctive, omni-directional crossed loop aerial mounted above the wheelhouse. The precursor to radar, the system's capabilities had their limitations. It was a passive system in that it could only pick up signals from radio beacons ashore, measuring the signal amplitude to get fixes on each station's bearing. By a system of triangulation, she could then plot her position with a fair degree of precision. However, the long-wave signals received over great distances were prone to atmospheric disturbances and could be influenced by the earth's curvature, affecting navigational accuracy. Consequently, the system's greatest effectiveness was to some extent limited to when the *Queen Mary* was within close range of land or in the approaches to port where short-wave signals were also transmitted.

Steering a course across the open ocean with confidence still in those days largely relied on the established practices of celestial navigation using sextants.

During the Second World War both the *Queen Mary* and *Queen Elizabeth* were fitted with their first radar installations, primitive instruments by today's standards. Essentially radar may be considered as an advanced form of active RDF. Where the latter had relied on the interception of signals broadcast from radio beacons, with radar the ship itself becomes both the transmitting and receiving station. The radiating electronic beam is reflected back from any metal object upon which it falls, each echo displayed on a cathode ray screen giving its bearing and range. While this did not aid the officers of the first Queens in fixing their position upon the ocean, it certainly assisted safe navigation, helping to prevent collisions on the busy sea-lanes and in poor visibility, while in wartime it enabled the identification of potentially hostile vessels that lay ahead in the ship's path.

The early radar installations of the *Queen Mary* and *Queen Elizabeth* were replaced with more and more progressive versions as they became available in the post-war years.

An essential item of equipment in the wheelhouse of the original Queens was their gyro-compass, their principal navigational aid. The *Queen Mary* was one of the first high-profile merchant ships to be equipped with such an instrument where previously most ships, other than warships, had been fitted with the magnetic compass alone. Whereas the magnetic compass depends for its action on the Earth's magnetism, the gyroscopic compass operates by the rotation of the Earth and the pull of gravity. Incorporating a continuously driven gyroscope whose rapidly spinning axis always indicates true North, irrespective of the ship's course or attitude, it is unaffected by either the Earth's or the ship's magnetic fields. Repeaters fitted in various parts of the ship are worked from a transmitter at the master compass. As an aid to navigation it was for long the principal means of confidently

ABOVE Compared to the bridge of the *Queen Mary*, that of the *Queen Mary 2* is totally different, dominated by computer screens and without a traditional ship's wheel to be seen. *Cunard*

ABOVE A general view of the central wheelhouse on the *Queen Mary*'s bridge. Despite its vintage appearance, the *Queen Mary*'s navigational gear embraced every refinement available at the time of her inception. *Andrew Kilk*

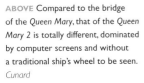

RIGHT The crow's nest high on the foremast of the *Queen Mary*. The sharp lookout of the seaman on watch from this lofty viewpoint was relied on for forward vision before the days of radar. *Shawn Drake*

determining the ship's course and heading and it remains a vital tool to this day, frequently linked to electronic systems receiving positioning data beamed from satellites. In fact, even in its infancy, the gyro compass was the core component of the so-called 'Iron Mike' or robotic navigator, an early form of auto-pilot.

Besides their gyro compasses, the *Queen Mary* and *Queen Elizabeth* also carried acoustic-electric fathometers and patent logs for measuring the daily distances run.

By the time the *Queen Elizabeth 2*, which had two Sperry Mk. 37 gyro-compasses, entered service in May 1969, the technology of electronic navigation had moved forwards in leaps and bounds. So too had the bridge accommodation itself. It would be an understatement to say the bridge spaces aboard the *Queen Mary* and *Queen Elizabeth* were at best rugged, inhospitable areas with bare teak decking underfoot and exposed deck-heads above, criss-crossed by pipework and cable runs. Even on the much later

---

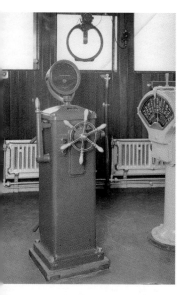

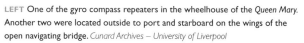

LEFT One of the gyro compass repeaters in the wheelhouse of the *Queen Mary*. Another two were located outside to port and starboard on the wings of the open navigating bridge. *Cunard Archives – University of Liverpool*

RIGHT Another photograph of an early radar installation aboard the *Queen Elizabeth* shows the displays housed in a specially-built enclosure in her wheelhouse. *Cunard Archives – University of Liverpool*

*Queen Elizabeth 2*, the bridge wings were still open to the elements. It has only been on the *Queen Mary 2* and the latest Queen cruise ships that the navigating bridge has been enclosed across its entire width, affording officers protection from the weather when manoeuvring in port or docking.

The bridge of the past gleamed with the polished brass of engine room telegraphs, ship's wheel and voice pipes, all features that have completely disappeared from the bridges of the modern Queens. Today, joystick controls have replaced the traditional ship's wheel, and the engine room telegraphs, once the only means of relaying speed and helm instructions below, have disappeared. Control of the Queens in every respect, from engines, steering and the monitoring of onboard safety systems now takes place on the bridge, rendering many of the instruments of the past redundant.

Though now broadened with other responsibilities, the Technical Department's role has changed as a consequence of these developments for, while engine monitoring is handled by the engineers in port, all running controls are transferred to the bridge prior to sailing.

Aboard the *Queen Mary 2, Queen Victoria* and new *Queen Elizabeth* the bridges are characterised by an array of

LEFT The initial radar equipment installed aboard the Queens during the Second World War was relatively basic in its performance. Nevertheless, it was essential for their independent troop dashes across the Atlantic in the run-up to D-Day. It was gradually superseded by improved equipment. The picture shows a radar scanner and associated equipment on the *Queen Elizabeth,* dating from the late 1940s or early 1950s. *Cunard Archives – University of Liverpool*

computer screens displaying navigational and chart information as well as diagnostic and status data for all vital onboard systems, a trend begun with the *Queen Elizabeth 2* in her Systems Safety Control Centre. No longer is there a need for a Quartermaster to take and carry out helm instructions. Now the officer of the watch can oversee and manage the ship's movement and behaviour from the comfort of a padded seat. There is even an auto-pilot system available, although it is always operated under the watchful eye of the duty officer. With digital electronics central to every function that is the responsibility of the Queens' Deck Officers, even the Chart Room has become obsolete, so that today the only spaces aboard the Queens that carry that name are luxury lounges located on the main public accommodation decks.

Similar to the original Queens and just as the latest Queens now are, the *Queen Elizabeth 2* was, in her day, a showcase of the most advanced navigation and safety systems so far developed. Among the ground-breaking appliances that were installed aboard the *QE2* was collision avoidance radar which could project her

ABOVE The sleek navigation mast of the *Queen Elizabeth 2* with SAM radar scanner. Her radar facilities included an Automatic Radar Plotting Aid (ARPA), a device which integrates and processes electronic data from radar, gyro compass and speed log sources. She was the first UK-registered passenger liner capable of navigating by a 4-point Satellite Navigation System, and she scored another first when, in July 1986, the first satellite transmission of a television programme from a merchant ship at sea was made from her. *Cunard*

ABOVE The sturdy navigation mast of the *Queen Victoria* bristles with radar scanners and radio antennae. *Author*

course plot forward relative to the tracks of nearby or approaching vessels and calculate the times to the closest safe passing distances or warn when an unsafe degree of proximity was likely to arise. She also had a computerised four-point satellite navigation system, among the earliest examples of its kind and a precursor to today's Global Positioning System (GPS).

A review of the navigational equipment installed aboard Cunard's present-day flagship *Queen Mary 2* provides a representative view of what is typically deployed aboard all three ships of the current Cunard fleet for safe running, course plotting and overall safety management.

The heart of the *Queen Mary 2*'s navigation facilities is the Multi-Function Screen Technology (MFST) system supplied by Kelvin Hughes. It employs eight work stations for the display and control of seven integrated processes. There are two for the electronic chart display and information system (ECDIS), four covering radar and one for dynamic positioning (DP). The latter uses various sensors such as wind speed and direction, heading and GPS speed to accurately predict the combination of pods and, when docking, bow thrusters required to maintain the required position. The DP system also allows control of the ship through a joystick.

The *Queen Mary 2* has five radar scanners, allowing complete 360-degree coverage. Covering both long and short range, they have a built-in Automatic Radar Plotting Aid (ARPA) permitting more than 40 targets to be tracked simultaneously. The course and speed of each target with the time to and its closest point of approach are instantly and continuously accessible, along with other collision avoidance information. Predictions on the behaviour of observed targets can be obtained should course changes be desired. Global Positioning System (GPS) satellite data is fed to the radars and ECDIS to ensure accurate course plotting and station-holding.

The navigation equipment includes a fully adaptive autopilot controlled by the ECDIS and compact voyage data recorder, somewhat like an aircraft's 'black box'.

ABOVE The telephone exchange aboard the *Queen Elizabeth* which, like that on her half-sister *Queen Mary*, was typical of any office switchboard ashore. Linking all the vital on-board service locations as well as the First-class staterooms, it had 700 lines. *Cunard*

ABOVE The *Queen Mary's* radio receiving room on her Sun Deck was approximately 250 feet forward of the radio transmitting room, their wide separation necessary to avoid interference. Radio Officers handled all of the ship's radio and telephone traffic as well as the navigation communications, including signals transmitted from RDF beacons.
*Cunard Archives – University of Liverpool*

A Computer Safety System (CSS) allows all safety systems throughout the ship to be monitored and provides a visual indication of any developing situation. It permits the operation from the bridge of watertight doors, fire screen doors, ventilation and low level lighting. Engine performance can also be monitored from the bridge, as can the ship's stability, with controls to adjust levels in the heeling tanks if required.

For weather forecasts, navigational information and warnings as well as for transmitting distress signals in an emergency, the *Queen Mary 2* is linked to the worldwide Global Maritime

Distress and Safety System (GMDSS) via two INMARSAT satellites, a development that has replaced the dedicated Radio Officer of the past.

The original *Queen Mary's* navigational tools may have been basic when compared with what is available today. So too, her communications equipment, though sophisticated by contemporary standards, now sounds distinctly vintage. One of her most innovative features was her radio telephony apparatus, by which passengers could ring and talk in complete confidence to anyone anywhere in the world who was linked to the

ABOVE The Connexions facility aboard the *Queen Mary 2* is more than another computer suite. It provides the means for running seminars and corporate presentations, utilising Internet connections for downloading up-to-the-minute data. Both the *Queen Victoria* and *Queen Elizabeth* have Connexions rooms. This is the highly ornate passageway outside the Connexions entrance. *Cunard*

service, book restaurant sittings, arrange hair salon appointments and generally exploit a range of hotel services connected to the facility. However, it should be borne in mind that it was exclusive to those booked in First-class, for only the staterooms in that category of accommodation were provided with receiver handsets.

Of particular mention was the *Queen Mary*'s broadcast wireless equipment which permitted radio programmes from land stations on either side of the Atlantic to be received and redistributed around the ship via clusters of loudspeakers, 38 in all, placed in key locations. The arrangement also allowed events such as orchestral performances that occurred in one part of the ship to be piped to other areas. Second and Third-class passengers may have been denied participation in a First-class ball but at least they could hear the music!

Wonders of their time, these facilities were replicated aboard the *Queen Elizabeth* and enhanced with early Public Address systems which, when not used for passenger announcements, were used for playing gramophone records. But how primitive these contrivances seem when compared with the telecommunications technology exhibited aboard the modern Queens.

Today, every single stateroom and cabin has a telephone, from which direct ship-to-shore calls can be easily made, and a television set with information channels covering onboard activities or previewing the highlights of ports of call on the ship's itinerary, besides looped videos and other programmes from the ship's own TV station.

Even those advances pale into insignificance now the possibilities of the computer and the World Wide Web have been exploited. Each of the latest Queens has a dedicated computer room for passenger use where, via Internet connections, websites may be readily accessed allowing banking transactions, online shopping and the sending and receiving of email messages. How marvellous it is that today's passengers can take digital photographs and video clips during their voyage and relay them

telephone networks. Much was made of the convenience of this telephone facility but calls had to be routed through the onboard exchange which, though as large as many ashore, required scheduling of ship-to-shore calls. Nevertheless, by an arrangement of two separate radio offices positioned wide apart on the *Queen Mary*'s Sun Deck, it was possible to transmit and receive simultaneously.

Besides calls to subscribers on land, the telephone system also permitted communication around the ship, allowing passengers to speak to friends and acquaintances, call for room

RIGHT The Computer Room of the new *Queen Elizabeth* where passengers can either receive tuition or book sessions for Internet browsing or the transmission and reception of emails. For those with personal laptop computer equipment, ship-wide connectivity permits these transactions to be performed in the privacy of staterooms. *Cunard*

to friends and family ashore even before their Queen has reached its destination.

One may easily form the view that the extraordinary array of navigational tools and communication systems at the disposal of the officers aboard the current generation of Queens may have compromised the seamanship skills on which past operation depended or, to some extent, has rendered them as obsolete, but not so. Cunard prides itself on having the most highly-professional Deck Department crews whose seamanship capabilities are second to none. Not only have those traditional competences been retained aboard Cunard's Queens but they are upheld in accordance with Company policy and the finest traditions of the British Merchant Navy. Forever the baseline, they are no more than complemented by the range of electronic facilities now available which are essentially seen as 'aids to navigation'.

However, just as for the Technical Department, technological advances, including a fair degree of automation, have had a direct impact on the staffing level of the modern Queen's Deck Department to the advantage of those departments caring directly for passengers. Both the total number of Deck officers and ratings, as well as the percentage of the total crew represented by the Deck Department, has more than halved.

LEFT Two of the large satellite navigation radomes on the cruise ship *Queen Elizabeth*. A third dome, mounted on a short mast, is located aft of her funnel. Each of the modern Queens carries a vast array of electronic navigation and telecommunication aids. *Author*

| DECK DEPARTMENT NUMBERS | | | |
|---|---|---|---|
| | **Queen Mary** | **Queen Elizabeth 2** | **Queen Mary 2** |
| Number | 190 | 62 | 66 |
| Percentage of total crew | 15 | 6 | 6 |

Photographed on 16 June 2007, the *Queen Mary 2* passes Cowes, Isle of Wight as she heads for the Spithead forts and the open sea. From every viewpoint, she is a most impressive ship. *Author*

# Bon Voyage

WHEN PASSENGER COMFORT ABOARD SHIP IS CONSIDERED, two concerns rank above all others as paramount. First undoubtedly is seasickness, or *mal-de-mer* as the French call it; an experience of sheer misery for those unfortunate enough to succumb to this dreadful affliction. Next most important must be the quality of the air inside the ship, especially when its operational sphere takes it to tropical climes.

Most ships have teething problems of one sort or another and the Queens have been no exception. One of the *Queen Mary*'s shortcomings when she first entered service was her tendency to roll, occasionally alarmingly. It was once said of her in those early years that "she was so tender, she would have rolled on wet grass". Another equally sardonic commentator quipped that the *Queen Mary* could roll the milk out of a cup of tea. The fact was that on one occasion she rolled over to 35 degrees! The result was a lot of broken crockery besides a few injuries.

A graphical description of how the *Queen Mary* could behave when big seas were encountered was related by the late Ron Winter when he described an experience he had while serving aboard her as a Junior Electrical Engineer. On this particular occasion he received orders to repair the electric heater in the crow's nest on her foremast. Having climbed to this lofty position, 130 feet above the waterline, where he inevitably took the opportunity to look out over the fore-deck, he became aware that, because of the acute perspective at that height, he could not see the mast by which he was physically attached to the ship itself. For all the world he felt as if he was in a crazy, low-flying aircraft. What made this sensation of detachment feel even more peculiar was the fact that, with the ship's extreme and ponderous roll, his 'aeroplane' seemed to be veering wildly from one side to the other, at one moment over the sea beyond the ship's hull on the portside and the next out to the same extent over the sea to starboard. Needless to say, the task in hand was completed as hastily as possible and he rapidly descended to the ladder entrance on B Deck and the marginally greater comfort of the main accommodation below.

The problem, it was discovered, was caused by the *Queen Mary* being top-heavy or 'tender'. The cure was to increase her metacentric height by adding weight in the form of greater water ballast in the lower part of her hull, thereby lowering her centre of gravity. This, with other measures, helped to attenuate the worst of her unpleasant motion characteristics but it wasn't until the 1950s that they were more effectively overcome by the installation of Denny Brown stabilisers.

Though not prone to rolling to the same degree, the *Queen Elizabeth* was the first of the original Queens to receive stabilisation equipment during her refit of 1955-1956. Two retractable blades were fitted on either side of her underwater hull. The *Queen Mary* received her stabiliser fin sets over the winter of 1958-1959 but, in both cases, the operating machinery encroached into the already restricted engineering spaces, proving the point that it is never as easy to install equipment retrospectively as it is to build it into the hull from the outset. Indeed, on the *Queen Mary*, with her greater number of boilers, the mechanism had to be mounted vertically rather than horizontally.

In the *Queen Elizabeth 2* and all successive Queens, stabilisers have been incorporated from new for the control of excessive lateral motion. Stabilisation equipment, like other hull enhancements on passenger ships, has been improved over the past forty years. Today, aboard the *Queen Mary 2*, *Queen Victoria* and new *Queen Elizabeth*, the fins are stronger and more responsive, and are

LEFT The *Queen Mary* photographed by an aircraft of Coastal Command pitching severely as she ploughed through mountainous seas while crossing the Atlantic as a troopship in May 1942. Waves break over her as high as her bridge and completely immerse her forward hull. One wonders how her military occupants coped with the effects of such violent motion. *Crown Copyright*

ABOVE Even with fin stabilisers fitted, the sea conditions can still cause extreme pitching motion as demonstrated here by the *Queen Elizabeth 2* as she takes a wave over her bow during an Atlantic crossing in 2008 in tandem with the *Queen Victoria*. *Cunard*

RIGHT One of the fin stabilisers of the new cruise ship *Queen Elizabeth* in its stowed position tucked into a recess in the ship's hull. *Cunard*

controlled by computers which measure the extent of the hull's movement and then adjust the fin angle accordingly to rapidly reduce rolling. In contrast to the stabilising fins of the first three Queens, those on the latest Queens are not retractable but fold into the ship's side when not in use.

Even with the latest systems, if the conditions are extreme enough, some movement, yawing, pitching and rolling or all three combined, may still be experienced. Each system has its

performance limits as well as its safe limits after which, if still deployed and the limits are exceeded, damage could result. However, it should be remembered that the weather behaviour typical of each modern Queen's sphere of operation has a bearing on the frequency of fin utilisation and the acuteness of the pitch settings required.

If motion attenuation is the primary consideration where passenger comfort is concerned, then air quality is definitely the second. The *Queen Mary* and *Queen Elizabeth*, built for transatlantic service alone, lacked sophisticated, comprehensive air conditioning systems although what they had was significantly in advance of the typical provision of the times, befitting their high-profile status. Wartime trooping, which took them to tropical climates, soon highlighted the inadequacies, however, for it could be unbearably hot down below for the men billeted in the former public spaces. Troops took to sleeping on the open decks, partly because of the cramped sleeping quarters and the enforced need for 'hot-bedding' but mainly for a measure of relief from the 'tween-decks heat.

The cruises of today's Queens, in fact those too of the *Queen Elizabeth 2* before 2008, routinely take them through and into near-

polar, temperate and tropical zones, necessitating comprehensive conditioning of air quality, temperature and humidity.

Returning to the *Queen Mary*, she had two systems installed providing a quite high measure of management of air quality, one of them a form of partial air-conditioning of her main public room areas. Also, in the passenger staterooms and cabins there was a forced-air ventilation system fed through punkah louvres set into the bulkheads and individually adjustable for direction and force. For the passengers in First-class there were also wall-mounted electric fans.

Though far from ideal, especially when she carried military personnel across the Indian Ocean and through the Red Sea, these provisions were otherwise generally adequate for the North Atlantic run and remained so until the early 1960s. But then both Queens were sent on cruises to such places as Nassau in the Bahamas in order to generate more revenue as their regular service traffic declined. What troops may have been obliged to endure, fare-paying passengers most certainly would not!

The *Queen Elizabeth*, having been earmarked to remain in service through to the mid-1970s with the imminent new *QE2*, was given a comprehensive ten-year, life-extending refit over 1965-66. Intended to fundamentally address some of the shortcomings that her revised function had emphasised, the modifications included the construction of a lido deck aft with an outdoor swimming pool while, notably, she had full air-conditioning extended throughout.

Since the introduction of the *Queen Elizabeth 2* in 1969, all Cunard's Queens have been fully air-conditioned, based upon the use of large chiller or refrigeration compressors circulating air maintained at an ambient temperature of around 23 degrees Celsius.

There is also the matter of passenger safety to consider and, in particular, how the designers and constructors of the Queens have provided for fire prevention and the protection of the ship in the event of a collision.

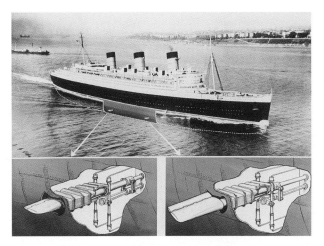

LEFT Intended primarily to control rolling rather than pitching, the *Queen Mary*'s fin stabiliser installation is depicted in this contemporary illustration, revealing how the fins telescoped outwards horizontally from their stowed position within the hull. *Cunard*

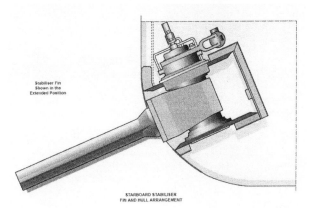

Stabiliser Fin
Shown in the
Extended Position

STARBOARD STABILISER
FIN AND HULL ARRANGEMENT

LEFT A cutaway view of the *Queen Victoria*'s starboard stabiliser. The fin swings outwards around a vertical axis from its stowed position, flat to the ship's side, out to its extended, deployed position. *Cunard*

Many exotic though highly flammable materials were incorporated into the public room decorations and furnishings of the *Queen Mary* and *Queen Elizabeth*. Moreover, besides the stateroom bed linen, curtains, drapes and carpets there were many other potentially volatile design fabrics. Few, if any, had fire retardant qualities and the prevention and containment of fire

LEFT Modern amenities for greater comfort aboard the original Queens, as revealed in this photograph of First-class cabin 115 on the *Queen Elizabeth*, include punkah louvres for ventilation and a wall-mounted fan. *Cunard Archives – University of Liverpool*

RIGHT The Systems Safety Control Centre of the *Queen Elizabeth 2*, a first for a sophisticated facility of this kind aboard a modern passenger ship. All vital systems and onboard services were monitored from this central location. *Michael Gallagher*

LEFT Today, the Cunard Queens have full air-conditioning throughout. In this view, taken of the lounge and dining area of the *Queen Elizabeth*'s Q2 Master Suite, the discreet air-conditioning grill can be seen above the sofa. The suite has fabrics and wall furnishings in subtle hues and a lot of space. *Cunard*

relied on the ship-wide smoke-detection sprinkler system and automatic fireproof doors that would seal off sections and compartments from one another in the event of an outbreak; also, regular fire drills as stipulated by the Board of Trade.

Since even before the emergence of the *Queen Elizabeth 2*, the pillaging of rain forests, which had reduced many tree species to endangered status, had reduced the palette of materials available to interior designers and with it some of the associated fire hazard. Equally, though, the marine industry's over-riding concern about the dangers of fire aboard ship had resulted in the embodiment of far more stringent regulations within the Safety of Life at Sea (SOLAS) conventions. As a consequence, the *QE2*'s fire avoidance standard was way ahead of that of the first two Queens. She had continuously-running fire pumps ensuring water was always available at sprinkler heads and fire hydrants and fire-fighting aids included foam, carbon dioxide and Halon.

Subsequent amendments to the SOLAS rules on fire prevention have taken the mitigation of fire risk even further such that today the *Queen Elizabeth 2* would fail the minimum mandatory requirements. On the *Queen Mary 2*, *Queen Victoria* and *Queen*

*Elizabeth* the very latest fire indication ('sniffing'), suppression and prevention systems are fundamental facets of their design and construction. All decorative materials and interior fittings now possess fire retardant attributes, while intensive and regular patrols and exercises involving the entire crew also ensure the highest level of safety and alertness at all times.

So, too, the structural integrity of the hulls of the latest Queens bears little similarity with that of the *Queen Mary* and *Queen Elizabeth* even though those Queens were, in their day, built to the highest, if not better than the highest, standards then prevailing. Like the present Queens, they had cellular double bottoms providing a continuous watertight skin, peak to peak, that also extended up their sides. Furthermore, an inner skin of steel plating in the engine room and boiler room oil bunkers plus transverse watertight bulkheads above the double bottom gave a high degree of hull compartmentation.

As safe as that sounds it pales by comparison to the watertight integrity of the latest Queens whose hull subdivision has been increased almost threefold to protect them should they be involved in a serious collision.

In place of the Winter Garden of the *Queen Victoria*, which has not proved as much of a success as its equivalent on the *Queen Mary 2*, Cunard have provided a Garden Lounge on the new *Queen Elizabeth*, its name a reference to a Third-class facility on the old *Queen Mary*. Light but sheltered, it is like a conservatory on the grand scale dominated by its radiating glass panels.
*Author*

# When Luxury Went to Sea

POSSIBLY THE MOST EVOCATIVE dimension of the Queens, when it comes to contemplating their standing as icons of luxurious travel at sea, is the design and decorative style of their accommodation, both in the public spaces in which passengers relax, mingle and socialise – the lounges, salons and ballrooms – and in the privacy of staterooms and cabins. Of course, the entire decorative scheme of each Queen's interiors has also encompassed their theatres and restaurants but these areas are dealt with separately in later chapters.

Before the emergence of the Queens, Cunard already had a reputation for the splendour of the interiors of its frontline ships, most notably those aboard the elegant *Aquitania*. The *Queen Mary* was conceived and constructed at a time when the vogue in ocean liner decorative fashion was in great flux. The gilded and filigreed Art Nouveau features of Palm Courts and Palladian Lounges had given way to the bold, geometric designs of the Jazz Age, influenced by such movements as the Bauhaus, Art Deco and Modernism and rendered in the modern materials of frosted and tinted glass, chromium and Bakelite. Having, through the financial difficulties brought about by the Depression, been pipped to the post by the French Line's *Normandie*, the most ostentatious showcase of modernistic décor, Cunard's quandary was whether to follow her lead and attempt to match the rival ship's exceptional lavishness or to opt for a more restrained style of decoration, still contemporary yet not so overpowering.

Just as he had been central in making the two-ship express service become a reality, so too Sir Percy Bates was there at the helm exercising a dominant, if controversial influence on the design of the *Queen Mary*'s interior, in effect reserving for the Cunard board the final say on what would or would not be entertained. Arthur Davis, a well-known designer of the London firm Mewès & Davis, was appointed as the coordinator of the project, although he was required to work in conjunction with the American interior design architect Benjamin W. Morris who had also been engaged. When this arrangement broke down through friction and Davis' ill health, Davis was replaced by his partner J. C. Whipp.

Sir Percy Bates' seemingly inflexible approach paid dividends, though, and the result, a muted version of the design vogue of the day, a unique and graceful style of décor, turned out to be well received, a vindication of his insistence on how it should look. It was at once variously described as 'Grand Hotel', 'Odeon', 'Cinema' or even 'the Cunard look', the latter an accolade of real distinction. Arising from the American contribution to its genesis, it drew on the perception of Britain and British culture as seen through the lenses of Hollywood moviemakers, slightly old-fashioned and whimsical but very stylish, and it exhibited features that were definitely 'Thirties' throughout its entire theme.

The restrained grandeur of the *Queen Mary*'s style was in marked contrast to some of the more extreme Art Deco opulence aboard the *Normandie*. A contemporary critic, rightly or wrongly summed it up by describing the *Queen Mary* as "the definition of elegance" while, conversely, the *Normandie* was criticised as having an "infection of ornamentation". To draw such a contentious conclusion, he could certainly not have been of French nationality and, taking a balanced view, his words did not reflect a unanimous opinion either.

Accusations were made in the trade press, however, that the *Queen Mary*'s decorative scheme was, in fact, rather a hotch-potch of different, incoherent elements lacking an overall theme but, on reflection, those criticisms seem to have

**LEFT** Taken from a booklet published in the 1950s to promote the *Queen Mary*, permitting an impression of her interiors in colour, this is the *Queen Mary*'s First-class Main Lounge. *David Hutchings*

**RIGHT** The 'A' Deck Lounge, a Second-class amenity, exhibited the *Queen Mary*'s characteristic style of décor. *Cunard Archives – University of Liverpool*

**ABOVE** Another booklet view, this is the Smoke Room, located athwartships on her Promenade Deck, aft of the Long Gallery. *David Hutchings*

been directed more at the artwork on display around the ship rather than at the furnishings and the overall decorative finish. The fact was that, having commissioned many of the leading artists and designers of the period, each of whom pursued their individual ideas, some of their work was subsequently rejected because Sir Percy Bates did not approve of it. Harshly, perhaps, he complained that some of the more explicit tableaux would be better removed and "given to the blind school".

Today, it is widely recognised that the *Queen Mary*'s interiors were superb and that she had a singularly distinct character and a unique grace and style. She may not have been 'avant-garde' but she was not intended to be. First and foremost, the *Queen Mary* had to be a comfortable means of transportation rather than a showcase of the creative possibilities of the modern age. Instead she offered a form of grandeur whose general ambience appealed to her passengers, the class of clientele which she had been designed to attract. A newspaper report published at the time of her maiden voyage aptly conveyed the image that had been carved for her:

 *The keynote is solid comfort and snugness characteristic of the best type of London or New York club where deep leather armchairs invite intimate conversations.*

Also that…

 *spacious beyond belief, her hospitality is yet warm and intimate",* while she had *"settings of exceptional splendour but without exaggeration.*

Most importantly, the *Queen Mary* introduced and established the style that was to become the hallmark standard expected aboard future Cunard Queens.

When the *Queen Elizabeth*'s interiors were finally unveiled in the mid-1940s they reflected a stronger British persuasion, though they were no more cutting edge than those of her older consort. Although she was referred to at times as "the beautiful

**LEFT** The sumptuous First-class Salon of the *Queen Elizabeth* presents a different style of grandeur, less 'Deco' and truly epic in its scale. The walls were of Canadian maple in a buff-pink shade. Decorations and upholstery in greys, blues and buff tones completed the colour scheme. *Cunard Archives – University of Liverpool*

**BELOW** The Third-class Lounge of the *Queen Elizabeth* offered comfortable seating and a reasonably large dance area. Music would have been 'piped' from elsewhere on the ship. *Cunard Archives – University of Liverpool*

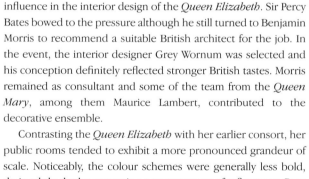

**ABOVE** The Second-class Lounge of the *Queen Elizabeth* is little different but does have its own piano for live concerts. *Cunard Archives – University of Liverpool*

lady" the *Queen Elizabeth* was also unjustifiably described in some quarters as the *Queen Mary*'s 'dowdy sister'. Nothing could have been further from the truth. Her public rooms took sophistication to new heights.

The British Government was keen to see less American influence in the interior design of the *Queen Elizabeth*. Sir Percy Bates bowed to the pressure although he still turned to Benjamin Morris to recommend a suitable British architect for the job. In the event, the interior designer Grey Wornum was selected and his conception definitely reflected stronger British tastes. Morris remained as consultant and some of the team from the *Queen Mary*, among them Maurice Lambert, contributed to the decorative ensemble.

Contrasting the *Queen Elizabeth* with her earlier consort, her public rooms tended to exhibit a more pronounced grandeur of scale. Noticeably, the colour schemes were generally less bold, their subtle shades conveying a greater sense of refinement. Rare veneers were again widely used throughout the ship and Formica was once more selected for the bathroom wall linings.

LEFT A very different style of décor is evident in this view of John Bannenberg's Double Room on the *Queen Elizabeth 2*. Reflective metal, plain dark laminated surfaces and a stark absence of ornamentation all contribute to an intensely minimalist feel. *Cunard*

RIGHT On the latest Queens, the cruise ships *Victoria* and *Elizabeth*, the Queen's Room, an essential feature since its introduction aboard the QE2, has taken the form of a classic ballroom with a gallery down one side and concealed seating areas. This is the Queen's Room of the *Queen Elizabeth*. *Author*

LEFT The First-class Queen's Room of the QE2, the creation of Michael Inchbold, offers a completely different interpretation of modern luxury. Serene and calming, accentuated by its fluted pillars and its broad airiness, it was finished in silver and white. *Cunard*

The solitary exception to the 'Cunard' style of interior was that of the unique *Queen Elizabeth 2* which, when she first entered service, featured a modernistic theme throughout in keeping with the spirit of the 'Swinging Sixties', the era in which she was conceived and designed. Her original design team was led by James Gardner and Dennis Lennon, who assembled a team of the leading interior designers of the day to produce a harmonised, strongly functional and contemporary representation of British national identity. Extensive use was made of laminates, Perspex, smoked glass and brushed and polished aluminium. An article in *The Times* aptly described her radical concept:

> *Moulded wood, wrought metal, folk weave and damask were out; plastic, stainless steel, tweed and leather were in".* Equally, *"green, brown and gold were out; oatmeal, sun yellow, dark blue and magnolia were in.*

Subsequently, through a succession of refits and overhauls, her décor evolved into a style that was closer to that seen aboard both the original and current fleet of Queen ships. At the outset, though, her internal design was progressive, even to some extent shocking as far as the purists or traditionalists were concerned. She was like a modern floating hotel at sea with jet-age facets to her interior arrangements. While some areas portrayed an exquisitely muted elegance such as Michael Inchbold's superb Queens Room, elsewhere, notably in some of the staterooms,

**LEFT** Some fifteen or more years have passed and, with the desegregation of the *Queen Elizabeth 2* to single class, the former Tourist-class two-level Double Room has been remodelled as the single-class Grand Lounge. Later, the forward end, where the gallery and the staircases descending either side of the orchestra pit can be seen, was modified to create a two-deck-high theatre stage suitable for cabaret shows. *Cunard*

**RIGHT** Entrance lobby design has undergone a considerable transition over the years, in some cases combined with the Purser's Office, in others with the shopping area and, more recently, as the focal point of a central atrium. On the original Queens there were three, one for each class. This is the First-class main entrance of the *Queen Mary*. On display are Maurice Lambert's polished-aluminium tablets symbolising progress of speed in various forms of motive power, entitled 'The Spirit of the Age'. *Cunard Archives – University of Liverpool*

**RIGHT** The Hall and Lobby of the *Queen Elizabeth* is reminiscent of the reception foyer of a grand hotel. *Cunard*

the design schemes were brash to say the least, characterised by the use of strong primary colours or harsh patterns. In those areas it was more Habitat and Pop Art than it was 'Mod'.

Conceived to appeal to a new, young-at-heart generation and to satisfy a sense of comfort that was equally apposite for both scheduled service voyages and cruise vacations, the *QE2* was unquestionably

LEFT Among the most refined settings aboard the *Queen Mary* were the Gallery Lounges on the Promenade Deck. Here is the Starboard Gallery situated between the Main Lounge and the Ballroom. *David Hutchings*

ABOVE More, rather harsh monochromatic décor on the *QE2* in the rather severe forward Lookout Bar and Observation Lounge, decorated in yellow and buff with dark blue leather furniture. This space was lost when the kitchens were expanded for the introduction of the Tables of the World Restaurant during a refit in the 1970s. *Cunard*

LEFT The striking red-carpeted Grand Lobby of the *Queen Mary 2*, located at the bottom of a six-deck atrium, has a completely unique style. It has a gallery at the level of the shopping area and glass-sided lifts. *Cunard*

ABOVE In the central lobby of the *Queen Victoria* the style has changed again, with sweeping stairs from several levels, intimate seating areas and a profusion of plants. *Author*

stylish. But she did not have the sweeping, grand rococo magnificence of her forebears or the compelling perspectives afforded by the open spaces and broad companionways of the new Queens. Despite her novelty, she offered luxury with simplicity and even a certain cosiness, reflected in a friendly onboard warmth which marked her out and made her especially popular with British passengers.

Alluding to the design influences of the era of her conception as well as to the conflict they aroused, according to the preferences of the critics, a *Daily Mirror* article provided a pertinently concise description of the *QE2*:

RIGHT The Midships Bar of the *Queen Elizabeth* aft of the Main Lounge, otherwise known appropriately enough as the Rose Lounge, was created during her winter refit of 1963-1964. It provided First-class passengers with a replacement for what had formerly been their exclusive Observation Bar overlooking the bows [see page 76], a public space that had been transferred to Third-class. *Phil Fricker*

ABOVE Distinctively furnished and illuminated, the Churchills Lounge of the *Queen Mary 2* typifies the modern cruise ship decorative style. *Cunard*

RIGHT The relaxing and sophisticated Chart Room of the *Queen Mary 2*. *Author*

" *She's a swinging super-ship, controversially beautiful.*

To assert, nevertheless, that she was majestic in her own way and still deserved recognition as a vessel of Queen ranking within a contemporary form of urbanity, the piece continued:

" *She has a regal beauty all of her own. It's there for all to see, built into her smooth and simple, sleek and graceful lines.*

Reaching back to the previous generation, each of the present Queens revives that renowned Cunard 'look' in its style and décor, or at least what may be regarded as a modern take on it. Today, though, while the interior designers have sought to perpetuate that fashion, they have augmented it with a lightness and airiness that modern materials and layouts have permitted, the result giving sumptuousness and grandeur a whole new meaning. Exploiting all the opportunities afforded by vast open spaces made possible by new construction principles and state-of-the-art propulsion systems, they evince a refinement and stylishness that is both grand and sophisticated, ornate yet not at all overpowering. Compared to other, contemporary passenger vessels they definitely have the 'wow' factor.

It is no accident that the *Queen Mary 2*, *Queen Victoria* and *Queen Elizabeth* should exhibit a version of the decorative style of the old *Queen Mary* and *Queen Elizabeth*. Cunard unashamedly trades on being British and on the grand heritage of its glorious past. Former President and Managing Director of Cunard Line, Carol Marlow, expressed it succinctly: "At Cunard, our history is really where our future lies".

The new *Queen Elizabeth* is a good example of this, her interior design intended to a degree to evoke those old transatlantic flyers. This has been achieved with iconic features sculpted in metal, glass and moulded plasterwork reminiscent of those on the *Queen Mary* and *Queen Elizabeth* and in the revival of fondly remembered passenger spaces like the Verandah Grill and the Midships Bar. She has been described, with some exaggeration, as "a cocoon of the past in which the clock has been turned back".

Many of the fine artworks that adorn the ship, selected under the stewardship of Amy Lucena, the Project Art Director, also conspicuously link the old with the new, such as the frieze in the Verandah Grill. It is an extract, surreptitiously but tastefully adapted, from Doris Zinkeisen's famous mural depicting a parade of circus characters, the full-size original of which, some 1,000 feet square in area, was the principal piece of decorative artwork in the *Queen Mary*'s Verandah Grill. Yet, as already stated, these design facets are embraced within surroundings that have a powerful aura of modernity, expressed

ABOVE 1930s-style ultra luxe accommodation aboard the *Queen Mary* – the sleeping area of First-class stateroom M50. Note how the portholes have been obscured by diffused transparent panels to soften the light and make the room's occupants feel less as if they are aboard ship. *Cunard Archives – University of Liverpool*

RIGHT Here lounge space has been taken al fresco in the form of the secluded Courtyard, an exclusive Grill-class facility adjoining the Grill Restaurants and abaft the Grill Lounge on Deck 11. It is a feature of both of the cruise ships *Queen Elizabeth* and *Queen Victoria*, this example being from the latter vessel. *Author*

ABOVE The *Queen Mary 2*'s Winter Garden is the modern equivalent of the Palm Court on Cunard steamers of the Edwardian era. With rattan furniture, slowly-rotating ceiling fans and an abundance of exotic potted plants, it suggests the orangery of a stately home. *Author*

in the openness and airiness of the ship's spacious interior where grand vistas abound.

Similarly, the *Queen Mary 2* evokes a strong feeling of nostalgia in her interior decorative schemes, recalling the great age of the transatlantic liners, yet through a deft and artistic amalgam of old and new she does not excessively look or feel old-fashioned and is very much a ship of her time. For her, bearing in mind her part-time transatlantic service, particular attention was given to the substance of the appointments and amenities of her top grades of accommodation, a key aim being to draw passengers away from the airliners operating that route.

The *Queen Mary 2*'s interior design was entrusted to Tillberg Design of Sweden. While to a large extent it reflects the current trends in top-class hotel design worldwide, embodied within it are countless references to Cunard's past in the transatlantic express service, among them cameos and hints of the Art Deco period in the form of reflecting chrome surfaces, mock wood-grain panelling, etched glass and geometric carpet patterns.

Cunard has appointed a Vice President of Interior Design, Teresa Anderson, who oversees the conception and fabrication of the interior architecture across the new Queens fleet focusing on carpets, tiles, curtains, panelling and light design. Concepts are realised under the guidance of Head Design Architects such as Giacomo Erasmo Mortola, whose company GEM was responsible for the *Queen Victoria*.

The transition of the accommodation aboard Cunard's Queens is concerned with more than just a simple comparison of splendour and scale. Equally important has been the layout of the passenger areas, a matter over which the evolution of the class system has had a major impact. Not only did this influence the allocation of space in each ship

BELOW The Lookout Bar of the past has been reprised as the Commodore Club aboard the *Queen Elizabeth*. Overlooking the bow, it offers comfortable seating in a relaxing location. *Author*

LEFT Many of the top class suites aboard the *Queen Mary* and *Queen Elizabeth* had delicately-grained wood panelling that can be best appreciated in this coloured view taken after the former ship's retirement at Long Beach. *Shawn Drake*

BELOW The double First-class bedroom of stateroom suite M69 on the *Queen Elizabeth*. The suite also had a private en suite bathroom and dining and lounge areas. *Cunard Archives – University of Liverpool*

ABOVE One of the spacious and well-appointed Grand suites of the *Queen Elizabeth 2*, number Q1. *Cunard*

LEFT The *Queen Mary 2*, like the cruise ships *Queen Victoria* and *Queen Elizabeth*, offers a range of exceptional top-grade suite accommodation. This is her two-level Balmoral Suite, one of five suites named after royal homes and palaces, located astern on Deck 10. *Cunard*

LEFT The incredible luxury of the private First-class suites of the original Queens can be fully appreciated in this view of the lounge area of suite M81 on the *Queen Mary*, exhibiting Art Deco features such as the mirror shape and the patterns of the carpet and rugs. The armchairs were upholstered in a rich shade of ultramarine blue. *Cunard Archives – University of Liverpool*

but it also determined how crew resources were distributed and what amenities the passengers in each class would or, conversely, would not enjoy in the confines of their private shipboard abode.

The *Queen Mary* and *Queen Elizabeth* were three-class ships throughout their entire careers. This meant that three grades of stateroom or cabin had to be provided and all the main public rooms, the restaurants and lounges, had to be triplicated. Of course there wasn't a straightforward repetition of these rooms at each level, nor were the facilities for each class of equal size. Those provided for the top class were a great deal more spacious and, as far as the lounges were concerned, there were generally more of them to choose from.

The class system also dictated the layout of the accommodation in another respect. The most comfortable spaces – those furthest

ABOVE The ultimate in suite accommodation aboard the *Queen Mary 2* are the twin Queen penthouse suites at the forward end of Deck 10 below the Observation Deck. This is the lounge area of the Queen Anne suite. Situated within the sloping front of her bridge structure, it overlooks the bow with uninterrupted forward views. *Cunard*

RIGHT Less capacious than the suites but still providing generous space and a high degree of comfort is this typical Balcony double stateroom number A3 on the *Queen Victoria. Cunard*

BELOW This is a double outside stateroom on the *Queen Elizabeth 2*, still impeccably maintained even though she was nearing the end of her career. The higher grades of accommodation aboard the Queens have been categorised as Grill-class since the *QE2* became, essentially, a one-class ship. The walls of the stateroom are clad with a specially-made, fabric-textured variant of Formica. Over 2 million square feet of the material was used on Cunard's third Queen. *Author*

from the engine noise and located where there would be less sensation of movement – were allocated to the premier class passengers. The Second and Third-class spaces were placed on lower decks and concentrated towards the bow and stern in a classic liner pattern, creating what was effectively a vertical or sliced disposition.

While not restricted exclusively for First-class clientele, the Promenade Deck of the *Queen Mary* serves to provide a good illustration of how, by class stratification, the prime areas were preserved for those paying the highest fares. It was very much a province of privilege, laid out within what were also exclusively First-class sheltered side decks. It comprised, from forward to aft, the Observation and Cocktail Bar, Studio, Lecture Room, Library, Drawing Room, Shopping Centre, Main Lounge, Long Gallery (portside), Ballroom, Starboard Gallery and Smokeroom. Passengers in the lower classes were excluded from these amenities by guarded or locked gates positioned at strategic points.

ABOVE This is one of the *Queen Elizabeth's* Third-class twin cabins that could be adapted to a triple-berth as shown here. Amenities remain basic in this inside cabin though it offers a measure of comfort with Korkoid composition flooring and rug. *Cunard Archives – University of Liverpool*

ABOVE The cruise ships *Queen Victoria* and *Queen Elizabeth* also have a selection of top-grade suites for discerning cruise voyagers. The bedroom of Princess Suite P1 of the *Queen Victoria* is seen here. *Cunard*

LEFT A Britannia Club double stateroom with balcony on the *Queen Elizabeth.* Outside staterooms without balconies are categorised as 'Oceanview'. *Cunard*

Although her passenger complement divided effectively into almost equal thirds by class, more than fifty per cent of the *Queen Mary's* interior space was allocated to First-class while in Third-class there was significantly less than a third of the space enjoyed by the top grade, much of it cheek-by-jowl alongside or amidst the crews' quarters.

Today, aboard the modern Queens, we take for granted having access to all the public rooms on the ship, excepting only the Grill Restaurants. Moreover, it is not regarded as anything unusual to have en-suite shower and toilet facilities in every stateroom and cabin, besides a telephone, a television, a mini-bar, a safe and a

LEFT Going back in time, the quality of the accommodation provided for lower-grade passengers aboard the original Queens was in most respects far superior to what generally was the standard of the day. Nonetheless, it was basic to say the least when compared with the equivalent accommodation today, lacking some essential amenities. This Second-class single inside cabin on the *Queen Mary* has only a wash-basin. The bathroom, and probably the toilet facilities, would have been communal, accessed along the companionway. Space, too, is at a premium. *Cunard Archives – University of Liverpool*

RIGHT Much the same is this convertible single or twin Third-class cabin on the *Queen Elizabeth*. Box-like and located in the part of the ship most affected by noise and motion, it would have been rather cramped for two passengers. It does, however, have louvred ventilation. *Cunard Archives – University of Liverpool*

host of other extras. Back in the days of the *Queen Mary* and *Queen Elizabeth* that was certainly not the case, such luxuries being very much limited to those in the top grade. The vast majority of Third-class passengers were obliged to use communal washrooms and lavatories for daily ablutions and calls of nature. Telephones, too, were only provided for passengers in First-class.

Where the accommodation layout aboard the first two Queens followed a vertical format, in the *Queen Elizabeth 2*, which finally

emerged as a two-class ship, the process of breaking down social barriers engendered the beginning of change in both the accommodation arrangement and the more efficient use of crew resources. The transition in distribution of the Queens' crews, owed partly to technological advances, was also the consequence of desegregation of classes as well as rising passenger expectations.

Where the numbers of Deck and Technical Department staff have more than halved, in excess of 85 per cent of the total crew

ABOVE Over the past fifty years, passengers in the lower fare categories have enjoyed far superior conditions as their accommodation has improved with the relaxation of the class system. This outside Mauretania-grade single cabin on the *Queen Elizabeth 2*, if no bigger than those on the *Queen Mary* and *Queen Elizabeth*, has all the creature comforts that characterised First-class accommodation in the past: it has a telephone and, out of sight, its own private en-suite shower room and toilet, plus an incongruously-placed television. *Cunard*

are now engaged in Hotel or Catering activities. For many passengers, however, these benefits have been enhanced by the fact that, through the eradication of the class system, these staff are no longer distributed across classes which would otherwise significantly reduce the crew to passenger ratio in the lowest categories of accommodation.

In passing, it is also interesting to note how, through the continuing metamorphosis of social change, the composition of the Queens' crews has changed with regard to both gender and nationality, having once been predominantly British and male. Union-Castle had introduced 'stewardettes', as they called them, a trend that was adopted aboard the *Queen Elizabeth 2*, launching a change whose momentum has seen the female element of the crew grow to the point where it now represents as many as 45 per cent of the total. How that contrasts with the *Queen Mary*, aboard which 94 per cent of the crew was male. It is much the same as far as the ethnic composition of the crew is concerned. On the first two Queens the crew was all but entirely British whereas, today, while the navigating officers remain mainly British, the rest of the crew is multi-national.

Looking at the accommodation distribution, certain public areas on the *QE2* remained devoted respectively to either First-class or Tourist-class, but the private accommodation was split along horizontal lines in classic cruise ship layout, with the most expensive accommodation placed highest. Like the *Queen Mary* and *Queen Elizabeth*, though, the recreational areas remained on upper decks with, apart from some minor exceptions, the staterooms spread out beneath them while none of the restaurants aboard these three ships was placed right aft.

Today shipboard layout has changed even more, driven by the cruise boom and the desire for as many passengers as possible to have outside cabins with balconies or verandahs. Hence, on the *Queen Mary 2*, *Queen Victoria* and new *Queen Elizabeth*, where class hierarchy has all but disappeared altogether, the public rooms and restaurants have been moved down onto lower decks

ABOVE Even on the *Queen Mary 2*, *Queen Victoria* and *Queen Elizabeth* the cabin accommodation at the lowest fare levels is adequate and comfortable if, perhaps, lacking in floor space. Air-conditioned with en-suite facilities, a safe, refrigerator, satellite television, data port outlet and telephone, this is a typical Britannia-class inside double on the *Queen Mary 2*. The stateroom can be made up as two singles, as shown here, or with a central double bed, as shown opposite. *Author*

and the passenger accommodation has been transferred to the highest decks, surmounted by the most lavish private suites. Some restaurants have been kept at a higher level – the *Queen Mary 2*'s Kings Court and the Lido and Grill Restaurants – but generally, the main restaurants are now located low down in the hull and the Britannia Restaurant on the *Queen Victoria* and *Queen Elizabeth* has been moved right aft extending across their full beam and affording views over the ocean for diners.

The main difference today, though, is that everyone has access to all areas and the attentions of the entire crew of each modern Queen are largely channelled to the benefit of all passengers irrespective of what they have paid for their ticket. The luxurious interiors and the exceptional service for which Cunard is renowned are now enjoyed by all.

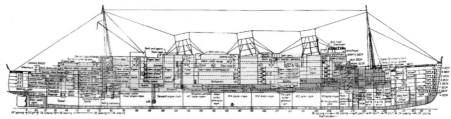

Queen Mary
  First Class – called Cabin Class from 1936-1947

  Second Class – called Tourist Class from 1936-1947 and renamed Cabin Class in 1948

  Third Class – called Third Class from 1936-1947 and renamed Tourist Class in 1948

**ABOVE** This view of an inside cabin on the *Queen Victoria* shows the central bed arrangement. While the bed may be large, the narrow access on either side testifies to the limited floor area, hinting, when compared to the expansive dimensions of the suites, at the disparity of space provision relative to fare that was a fundamental aspect of the segregated passenger accommodation on the original Queens. It should be remembered, though, that modern passengers have the run of virtually the entire ship, a dimension denied to their counterparts of the past. *Author*

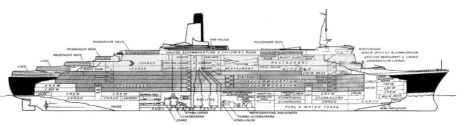

Queen Elizabeth 2
  Suites, Staterooms & Cabins

  Public Rooms & restuarants

**RIGHT** The accommodation distribution has changed from vertical to horizontal as these side elevations of the *Queen Mary* and *Queen Elizabeth 2* reveal. Further changes have seen entertainment spaces moved from high up to low down, as shown on the *Queen Mary 2*.

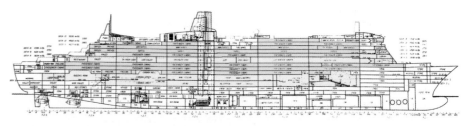

Queen Mary 2
  Suites, Staterooms & Cabins

  Public Rooms & restuarants

The *Queen Elizabeth 2* floodlit while berthed at Oslo during a 'Winter Markets' cruise in December 2007. By this time in her career she was virtually a diplomat ship for Great Britain, welcomed and admired everywhere. *Author*

# Cities at Sea

"WATER, WATER EVERYWHERE AND NOT A DROP TO DRINK", so the words of Coleridge's poem attest, hinting at the severe constraints on water supply from which many ships have suffered despite being surrounded by sea water on all sides as far as the horizon. Similarly, on a list of what purported to be the silliest questions ever asked of Cunard ship personnel was an apparently innocent enquiry from a passenger clearly inexperienced in maritime matters: "Does the ship generate its own electricity?" as if to suggest that a mini power station mounted upon a barge and connected by cables was towed along in the ship's wake, though somehow it was never there to be seen in daylight hours.

Great passenger ships, like all ocean trading vessels, are self-contained entities. Apart from food and fuel, virtually everything else consumed on board has to be produced on board. In particular, electricity for lighting, cooking, operating lifts and, in emergency, to work pumps and lifeboat davits; and water for washing, drinking, cooking, sanitation and fire-fighting systems and, on steam-driven ships, for the boilers to generate steam for the main engines. The larger and faster the ship, the greater the demand for these essential services and Cunard's Queens were and are no exception. Equipped with extraordinary production capabilities, they may be regarded metaphorically speaking as veritable cities at sea.

On the original Queens, both built as steamships, water was a particularly precious commodity. In the days of the express transatlantic service, thirsty boilers fired up to super-heated temperatures consumed vast volumes of water at the very same time as the fare-paying clientele, especially those who had booked in the most expensive suites and staterooms, made great demands on the supply of water over the course of a five-day voyage. Evaporators allowed the replenishment of tanks filled at Southampton and New York but it was certainly not the done thing to stint on how much fresh water top-class passengers were permitted to use. Nor to deny sufficient quantities to the chefs who needed it for the preparation of the gourmet cuisine for which the Queens were renowned. Down below, in the engine rooms, desalination plants produced around 300 tons daily of softened boiler feed water, while condensers helped to recirculate evaporated steam but leaking valves and glands always meant that what was carried steadily reduced as the passage proceeded. And, of course, the fog horns, sounded by the first two Queens whenever they were arriving or departing, or if beset by poor visibility, also relied on steam for their operation. As a consequence, there was a measure of rivalry between the different engine room departments to obtain sufficient of this essential consumable.

Mervyn Pearson, once a member of the engine room crew of the *Queen Mary*, relates a story pertaining to the persistent competition for fresh water that pervaded the ship's operation which may well be an urban myth but which nevertheless makes interesting, even humorous reading. So intense, apparently, was the struggle to satisfy the ship's conflicting needs that secretly, or at least so it was thought, the opposing engine room divisions – those running the main engines and those responsible for passenger services – were instructed by their respective chiefs to plumb lengths of pipe down in the bowels of the ship to syphon off the other's water supply. As both sections set about this act of chicanery in parallel, the result was no more than a lot of wasted effort in this microcosmic exercise in hydrology while the water which was central to the respective plots was simply pumped around in a loop.

To ease the demand on available fresh water, the bathrooms aboard the first two Queens were fitted with four taps, two to supply hot and cold fresh water and two

for hot and cold salt water, while the swimming pools were also filled with the latter. Much was made of the efficacious qualities of salt water for toning passengers' bodies and skin, no doubt enthusiastically endorsed by the bathroom steward with whom baths were booked and who was responsible for issuing bars of salt-water soap.

Particular pressure in respect of water consumption was experienced by the *Queen Mary* and *Queen Elizabeth* during their wartime careers as troopships, simply because, on most ocean crossings, their passenger complements had more than quadrupled. Far fewer baths may have been taken but there was still the need to serve the showers and there were a lot more men who needed drinking water, besides many more meals to cook. It can only be assumed that a strict regime of water rationing was enforced.

Today, it is expensive to take potable water by standpipe from the quayside and the modern Queens have both excellent production facilities and plentiful storage capacities.

An equally important commodity, both for the benefit of the passengers and to run all the on-board systems, is electricity. It is hard to imagine what it must have been like aboard an ocean packet before the days of electricity when the fire risk, from tallow candles and oil lamps, as the only means of light below deck, was a constant and major concern.

The possibilities that electrical power offered were exploited to the full on the original Queens. For instance, the *Queen Elizabeth* had 35 elevators connecting her 14 decks. Among other innovations conceived exclusively to enhance passenger comfort was electrically-heated towel rails installed in the cabins and staterooms.

As cities at sea, it has been necessary to provide the Queens with the means of dealing with other by-products of human consumption on a grand scale – the processing and disposal of waste of all descriptions and forms. On the three modern Queens, a great deal of effort has been taken to meet the modern environmental standards that are now mandated for ocean-going ships. To that end Cunard has developed a comprehensive environmental management system, certified to ISO 14001.

Each Queen has advanced equipment for the treatment of both effluent and fluid waste in order to reduce pollution. As far as the sanitation provisions are concerned, with so many people to cater for they are highly complex. Suffice to say that adequate secure storage facilities have been provided aboard the Queens and, during port turnarounds, the remaining, processed contents are removed ashore. Waste water is processed using Membrane

## WATER PRODUCTION SYSTEMS

The table compares the potable water production systems, production volumes and storage capacities of each of the Queens.

| | Production System | Daily Production Volume | Storage Capacity |
|---|---|---|---|
| **Queen Mary** | 4 × evaporators | 400 tons | 468 tons |
| **Queen Elizabeth** | 4 × evaporators | 400 tons | ca 470 tons |
| **Queen Elizabeth 2** | 4 × flash distillation evaporators plus reverse osmosis unit | 1,200 tons increased to 1,450 tons | 1,852 tonnes |
| **Queen Mary 2** | 3 × multi-effect plate evaporators | 1,890 tons | 3,525 tons |
| **Queen Victoria & Queen Elizabeth** | 3 × flash low-pressure six-stage evaporators | 1,700 tons | 3,152 tons |

*Notes*

Daily fresh water consumption aboard the *Queen Mary 2* is estimated at 1,100 tons, equal to 302 litres or 79 US gallons per person

For approximate conversion 1 tonne = 287 US gallons = 1.085 m3 and 1 metric tonne = 0.9842 UK (long) tons or 1.1023 US (short) tons

## ELECTRICAL GENERATING SYSTEMS AND POWER OUTPUTS

This table contrasts the electrical generating systems and power outputs of each Queen.

| | Generating System | Total Power Output | Propulsive Power Consumption |
|---|---|---|---|
| **Queen Mary** | 7 x turbo-generators | 10.0 MW | n/a |
| **Queen Elizabeth** | 2 x turbo-generators | 8.8 MW | n/a |
| **Queen Elizabeth 2** *(as a steamship)* | 3 x turbo-generators | 16.5 MW | n/a |
| **Queen Elizabeth 2** *(as a diesel ship)* | Coupled GEC diesel generators | 94.5 MW | 44.0 MW |
| **Queen Mary 2** | Main engines* | 117.2 MW | 86.0 MW |
| **Queen Victoria & Queen Elizabeth** | Main engines* | 63.4 MW | 35.2 MW |

Notes

*The *Queen Mary 2* has integrated combined diesel and gas turbine generators (CODAG); the *Queen Victoria* and *Queen Elizabeth* have integrated diesel generators

n/a = not applicable

Biological Reactors. The filtered output is sufficiently clean to be suitable for use with certain auxiliary systems. The residue, like effluent, is discharged in port in a non-toxic form for disposal in accordance with the latest regulations.

In passing, an interesting story underlines the extraordinary lengths that Cunard staff were prepared to go to in the service of their valued passengers. Chief Mechanical Engineer Brian Atkinson, once of the *Queen Elizabeth 2*, recalls how on more than one occasion lady First-class passengers lost valuable small items of jewellery down the sink in their bathrooms while readying themselves for the evening functions. More than happy to oblige, upon the request of the skipper of the day, Brian and his team would drain down and filter the appropriate septic tank and more often than not manage to retrieve the errant gemstones, to be returned after careful cleaning. However, they did draw the line when they were informed that a certain

gentleman passenger suffering from sea-sickness had lost his false teeth down the toilet!

In the past, the ocean was not exactly treated as a convenient dustbin but an awful lot of food and other waste was routinely jettisoned over the side. It was said that the flocks of seagulls that followed in the wake of the ocean liners testified to the epicurean plenitude of the scraps discarded into the sea but the most discerning gulls were surely those that followed Cunard's Queens. Today, not only is such a form of waste disposal frowned upon but it would contravene the regulations that now seek to protect and conserve the world's oceans and the life systems that depend upon the preservation of their purity. As with effluent, general rubbish is now discharged in a conveniently treated form for recycling onto waiting barges that have been summoned ahead by communication to the appropriate department of Carnival Operations.

**ABOVE** There was no such choice to concern passengers travelling in Third-class and even some of those whose accommodation was Second-class cabins. As shown in other Second and Third-class cabins, there is only a wash basin in this three-berth cabin on the *Queen Mary*. Such conditions were far removed from the luxury of a steward-filled, steaming hot bath. *Cunard Archives – University of Liverpool*

Grill Restaurants have continued to be an essential constituent of the dining options offered aboard Cunard Queens for top-grade passengers but from the inception of the *Queen Elizabeth 2*, one of whose three Grills is depicted here, their names were prefixed 'Princess', 'Queens' and 'Britannia'; also latterly the meal costs were incorporated in the ticket price. More spacious than the Verandah Grills of the original Queens, an avant garde decorative style has been adopted in place of the plush interiors of the past. *Cunard*

# Food, Glorious Food

CULINARY EXCELLENCE HAS BEEN ASSOCIATED with the Queens from the outset but it could be said that it was more of a consistently very high standard rather than exceptional. Back in 1935, Sir Percy Bates had sought advice from Mr. Rupert D'Oyly Carte of the London Savoy as to how he could achieve the epicurean status he desired for Cunard's prestigious new flagship. The guidance he offered was not altogether as expected:

> " *There are no super-restaurants; only good, moderate or bad. What is wanted is a really good restaurant with really well-cooked food, not necessarily enormous variety as the trip is short, and really good service.*

That advice was reflected in the Queen Mary and it set a standard that has been pursued ever since. Today, the quality of every aspect of catering aboard the Queens is maintained under the stewardship of a roving Cunard World Culinary Ambassador, Michelin Star Chef Jean-Marie Zimmerman. He spends time aboard each vessel of the present fleet, developing new menus and ensuring that the standard of cuisine demanded by the Cunard operation is unerringly maintained at the highest level.

Essentially, the scene in any of the galleys aboard the modern Queens is little different from what would have been found aboard the first generation of these great liners when they were working the North Atlantic Run.

There may be fewer persons engaged on the food preparation side of the catering operation these days but there is the same bustle and energy culminating in a near frenzy of activity as meal times approach. Bernhard Stumpfel, Executive Chef aboard the *Queen Victoria*, euphemistically describes it as "well organised chaos". But there is no shouting, no aggravation or antipathy between those involved, only the noise of a well-oiled machine going about its routine. For it is true to say that the qualities which underpin the Queens' high standards of gastronomic excellence of today are no different from those of the past: exceptional skill, broad experience, good management, perfect timing and a measure of human psychology.

The kitchen equipment has, of course, improved enormously when compared with what was considered cutting edge 75 years ago, even if it is not quite so robust. As Bernhard Stumpfel explains, it is no longer simply "On or Off" or "Up or Down". The controls are more sensitive and the heat sources more responsive but what really makes it possible to deliver haute cuisine food on the scale achieved aboard Cunard's Queens – from 800 to 1,250 meals at a sitting (35-45,000 total meals on a typical 5-day Atlantic crossing) – is the dedication and professionalism of the galley team. It is a happy team where, despite the pressure of constant demand, there is good humour and mutual respect between the team players, and that, no doubt, was how it was in the past.

A key ingredient to the ability of producing the right number of high quality meals every time based on each day's menu selections, with the minimum of wastage, is the Executive Chef's astute ability to predict. It may be thought that

LEFT The magnificent, high-ceilinged First-class Restaurant of the *Queen Mary*. Capable of accommodating 800 persons at each sitting, during the Second World War it was filled with multi-tiered standee bunks as the sleeping quarters of thousands of GI's. *David Hutchings*

RIGHT The Second-class Restaurant on the *Queen Elizabeth*, though of smaller proportions than that in First-class, seated a similar number of diners. *Cunard Archives – University of Liverpool*

ABOVE Less grand but still comfortably, if not luxuriously, appointed for its category is the Third-class Dining Saloon on the same ship. *Cunard Archives – University of Liverpool*

determining the quantities to be cooked relies on good, old-fashioned intuition but, in fact, it draws on empirical wisdom and a measure of help from a computer. We live today in a global community, a matter reflected in the diverse nationalities of the Queens' passengers, each with their own tastes and preferences where food is concerned. On a transatlantic voyage in the 1930s it could have been almost guaranteed that the vast majority of those persons travelling on the *Queen Mary* would have originated from either the United States or the British Isles, simplifying the process of forecasting meal choices. Not so today; the modern-day Queens must satisfy a multi-national diet.

The Maitre d' has a computer system containing exhaustive details on each passenger: their gender, nationality, age, dietary constraints and so on, along with a daily meal count, information that is fed to the Executive Chef who, drawing on years' of understanding of tastes and eating habits and maybe using a bit of 'nouse', will determine in advance the quantity of each dish that should be prepared. His hit rate is an astonishing 90 to 95 percent. When put to the test, Bernhard Stumpfel was able to guess accurately every one of my selections from a typical five-course menu.

There is a legendary accolade pertaining to the culinary performance of the Queens' Chefs to the effect that they could produce anything a passenger wished for at any time, whether or not it was on the menu. The slogan was "Eat what you like, when you like and as much as you like". That may or may not have been the case in the past but it would be true to say that, given the opportunity, even today the Queens' Chefs will rise to such a challenge. Bernhard Stumpfel relates an incident along those lines: A guest arrived at the entrance to a restaurant on the *QE2*, placed a plastic bag on the reception desk and asked if his party could have the contents for dinner, prepared in any way the Chef suggested. Inside the bag was a very large breadfruit. After some discussion, it was decided to prepare two breadfruit curries – one green, one red – both well received but among the most unusual meals Bernhard's team had ever prepared.

Today, given that the sphere of operation of the Queens is dramatically different, exemplified by much longer voyages over immense distances, the ability to deliver such a consistently high standard of cuisine has had, by necessity, to adapt to the logistical difficulties involved. It is one thing to be able to carry a vast diversity of fresh produce over a five-day Atlantic crossing, quite another to cater for the victualling requirements of ocean legs three times as long on the far side of the globe.

Certain commodities present enormous problems – soft fruit, for instance, which will perish within twenty-one days and whose growing season is limited to brief periods of the year. On the plus side, though, modern refrigeration techniques and practices have made it possible to store such things as fish and meat for longer periods with little or no adverse effect to their flavour or texture. To preserve the flavour of fish, it is frozen after being steeped in sea water rather than fresh water.

On longer cruises, arrangements are made to ship ahead containers of frozen food as well as other perishables to permit replenishment of stocks at future ports of call, but here, too, there are restrictions which have to be taken into consideration. Federal regulations now prohibit the import of foreign meat into the United States of America as just one example. This includes sausages, which because the Queens no longer have butchers in the Catering team are no longer made on board.

Former Princess Grill Manager on the *QE2*, Jonathan Norton, tells how, through discreet observation of passenger eating habits on world cruises, the novices could be readily distinguished from the seasoned voyagers. Those taking a more than 90-day trip around the globe for the first time tend initially to overindulge at every mealtime which, along with a reciprocally low level of physical activity, could not be sustained. The more experienced adopt a restrained approach to food consumption from the first day, given that, with such appetising largesse, there is a long way to go.

There is probably no equivalent ashore to the scale of catering that is found aboard the Cunard Queens. Not only are huge quantities of servings of the finest cooking prepared for each mealtime but this could be taking place while the ship is moving in a turbulent seaway although it is probable that, in such circumstances, there would be fewer diners.

Organisation of the galley teams and, with it, the allocation of the planning and execution of key activities plays a large part in the

ABOVE During her refits, the restaurants on the *QE2* were gradually remodelled and renamed. Styled as the Mauretania Restaurant in this picture, this was formerly the Tables of the World Restaurant and, before that, the Britannia Restaurant. *Author*

ABOVE The Columbia Restaurant, which was originally the *Queen Elizabeth 2's* main First-class dining venue, located on her Quarter Deck, later became the Caronia Restaurant as shown here. Entered via a raised platform with short flights of stairs to left and right, it did not project the stunning grandiosity of the stylish entrance to the later *Queen Mary 2's* Britannia Restaurant. *Cunard*

ABOVE Here is the incredible Britannia Restaurant of the *Queen Mary 2*, its scale and magnificence hard to capture in a single photograph. As with the original Queens, its layout has been optimised by opening it up through almost three decks. The lower seating, on Deck 2, is overlooked by a split-level balcony on the higher deck. Crowned by a cupola of coloured glass, a reminder of the ornamental skylights of Cunarders of the past, it has an amazing capacity of as many as 1,347 diners. *Cunard*

LEFT A popular Lido restaurant along with a Club of that name was introduced aboard the *QE2* in the 1980s, taking the place of the old Q4 Room. This dining facility was revived on the *Queen Mary 2* in the form of the far more ambitious Kings Court, a buffet-style lido by day that converts into four themed restaurants at night. This is the Carvery. *Cunard*

ABOVE Arranged over two decks, the Britannia Restaurants of the *Queen Victoria* and *Queen Elizabeth* have a glittering gracefulness, characterised by gleaming chromium surfaces and laminated wall panelling in warm wood-grain shades, the decorative option that has replaced real wood veneers in an age of environmental and fire-safety awareness. Placed low down, right aft across the full beam of each ship, on Decks 2 and 3, diners have all-round views of the ocean. This photograph was taken aboard the *Queen Victoria*. *Author*

ABOVE Both the *Queen Victoria* and *Queen Elizabeth* have large Lido Restaurants which, like the *QM2*'s Kings Court, are placed high up, in their case on Deck 9. Contrasting with the formality of the Britannia and Grill Restaurants, Cunard have recognised that the modern passenger has a preference for a more casual dining option for breakfasts, lunches and even certain evening meals. This is the *Queen Victoria*'s Lido restaurant looking aft on the port side. *Author*

successful delivery of food in the required quantities. Aboard the *Queen Victoria*, and similarly on the new *Queen Elizabeth*, there are 145 Chefs and 63 galley utility staff, the latter comprising cleaners, dishwashers, sanitation officers and personnel dedicated to operating toasters and preparing hot drinks. The hierarchy of the Kitchen team cascades down from the Executive Chef to a single Executive Sous Chef, an Executive Pastry Chef, four Chefs de Cuisine, and nine Sous Chefs. Below the Sous Chefs are Chefs de Parties, Demi Chefs de Parties and Commis de Cuisine. The Chefs de Parties occupy key positions, each being responsible for the cooking of a different commodity: meat, fish, vegetables and so on. Of course, aboard the *Queen Mary 2*, with her greater passenger complement, the number of galley staff is proportionately higher.

To ensure all food is ready to be served at Restaurant times, there are night staff who commence food preparation for the following day. The Chefs start final meal preparation around one and a half hours before each Restaurant sitting begins.

For the passenger, the quality of the food is only half the experience of fine dining aboard a Cunard Queen. It is also about how the food is served, the attentiveness of the waiters, the range and vintage of the wines selected, assisted by the courteous but expert guidance of experienced sommeliers, and the general ambience of a well-run, relaxing restaurant setting. All this is down to the parallel team of the Catering Department, the team of waiters organised under the attentive oversight of the Maitre d' and his Assistant. In total, aboard the *Queen Mary 2*, the Restaurant Department comprises 297 people, among them 140 Waiters or Junior Waiters and 22 Wine Stewards all supervised by 9 Head Waiters.

Over the years, the arrangement of the kitchens on Cunard's Queens and the passengers' choice of restaurants have evolved considerably as the relaxation of segregation into classes gathered momentum. On the *Queen Mary* and *Queen Elizabeth* there were four kitchens, each adjoining one of the ship's restaurants. First-class passengers could dine in either the Main Restaurant or the Grill Restaurant, the Queens' Verandah Grills being world-famous for the standard of food they served. An interesting feature of the First-class restaurants aboard both the *Queen Mary* and *Queen Elizabeth* were the four anterooms, two large and two small, positioned at the corners of the main dining saloon on C deck, that could be reserved for private dinner parties and special occasions.

The Second-class Restaurant was the only dining option for passengers of that category, as was the Third-class Dining Room for those in the lowest grade of accommodation, the former abaft and the latter forward of the First-class Restaurant on the same deck.

When the *Queen Elizabeth 2* came out in 1969, it was decided that all meal preparation areas should be rationalised into a single large centralised kitchen serving all her restaurants which were clustered together around the forward end of the accommodation block. Minor food outlets elsewhere had their own pantries. The change to a two-class standard of accommodation simplified arrangements somewhat and the process of democratisation allowed all passengers some increased choice when it came to deciding where they should eat. There remained, however, considerable duplication of

**ABOVE** The Verandah Grill of the *Queen Elizabeth*, like that of the *Queen Mary*, had a raised and balustraded platform with piano for light musical entertainment. Where purple and white had been the colour scheme on the *Queen Mary*, the *Queen Elizabeth's* Grill had ivory-coloured, sycamore-panelled walls and the furniture was upholstered in pale blue. *Cunard Archives – University of Liverpool*

**ABOVE** Since the 1930s, the Cunard Queens have been famed for their a la carte Verandah Grills, exclusive First-class dining rooms that doubled as cocktail bars and night clubs after dark. All tables had to be booked in advance and meal costs were in addition to voyage fares. With 22 deep windows overlooking the aft Sun Deck, the decorative style of the Grill aboard the *Queen Mary* typified the blend of luxury, tradition and contemporaneity which Cunard had consciously sought to appeal to the 80 per cent or more American passengers who dominated the Atlantic trade. *David Hutchings*

facilities and staff resources. The transition to cruising gradually led to the *QE2* becoming effectively a single-class vessel. Restaurants were revamped, renamed, relocated and, apart from her selective Britannia, Princess and Queens Grills, were open to all regardless of the level of their cabin accommodation or ticket price. And that, more or less, is how dining aboard the Queens is arranged to this day.

Now there are more restaurants to choose from, typically the featured multi-level Britannia Restaurant, the Todd English, the buffet-style Lido Restaurant and the Queens and Princess Grills which remain exclusive. Aboard the *Queen Mary 2*, in place of a Lido Restaurant, there is the King's Court which offers four themed sub-restaurants, while on the new *Queen Elizabeth* the Todd English has given way to the re-introduction of the famed

RIGHT A la carte dining on the modern Queens has taken the form of the select Todd English Restaurant where exceptional food and a chic ambience can be enjoyed for a surcharge. This view shows the reception lounge of the 216-seat Todd English of the *Queen Mary 2*. *Cunard*

ABOVE Besides the Todd English, the *Queen Mary 2* has her Grill Restaurants, giving her eight main eating venues. This is the Queens Grill. *Cunard*

LEFT Offering equally elegant surroundings for a fine dining experience, this is the Todd English on the *Queen Victoria*, its entrance located at the portside corner of the Grand Lobby on Deck 2. *Author*

Verandah Grill, one of the most elegant dining rooms on any modern cruise ship. Apart from the main restaurants there are other locations where light food is served such as the Cafe Carinthia, the Commodore Club and the Golden Lion Pub, all of which may be patronised by all passengers. Formal dress code remains the style of preference in the main restaurants and Grills aboard the Queens.

An examination of the crew resources in the Catering Department reveals an interesting trend. It has already been shown that the exploitation of modern technology for the power and navigation systems has led to reductions in Technical and Deck personnel which have bolstered the numbers employed in the Hotel and Catering Departments. Further analysis shows that the increase has been noticeably greater for those involved in food and beverage service (*see opposite*).

In the current fleet of Queens, the layout of kitchens has gone full circle, with the galleys once again distributed around the ships, each located as close as possible to the restaurant for which it is catering. The numbers have inevitably risen as a consequence, up to ten on the *Queen Victoria* and all run by a team of just 208 persons!

Scrutinising the lists of items victualled for a five-day transatlantic voyage, it is evident that there is not a great deal of difference between that of the old *Queen Mary* and *Queen Elizabeth* and that of the *Queen Mary 2* as recently as 2009. There are perhaps fewer exotic items these days and a greater reflection of the multi-national mix of the passengers but the range of commodities and the quantities are comparable.

Most striking is the size of the lists. For the *Queen Mary 2* there are 660 food items and, in the Beverages List, 190 drink and tobacco items. Among the Food List items, in summary, are 56,000 lbs of fresh vegetables, 21,000 lbs of fresh fruit, over 6,000 lbs of cheese of 35 types, 12,000 lbs of fish and almost 38,000 lbs of meat and poultry. There are 9,400 individual cartons of cereal, 63,000 tea bags in 14 different flavours, 1,150 lbs of coffee, either ground or as beans, 2,250 lbs of sugar and 1,265 gallons of fresh milk. Pasta of 17 varieties weighs in at 1,150 lbs.

Likewise, on the Beverages List there are in excess of 10,000 bottles or cans of beer and lager plus an additional 70 kegs containing 610 gallons. Cider drinkers are provided for by over 1,100 bottles. For the bars there are also 1,392 litres of spirits and 222 bottles of champagne, while primarily for consumption in the restaurants there are no fewer than 6,270 bottles of wine.

| STAFF DISTRIBUTION IN THE HOTEL & CATERING DEPARTMENT | | | | | | |
|---|---|---|---|---|---|---|
| | Queen Mary | | Queen Elizabeth 2 | | Queen Mary 2 | |
| | Staff | % of total H&C | Staff | % of total H&C | Staff | % of total H&C |
| Hotel | 465 | 56 | 482 | 56 | 341 | 35 |
| Catering | 364 | 44 | 378 | 44 | 635 | 65 |

ABOVE The forward Observation Bar on the *Queen Elizabeth*, the popular evening rendezvous for First-class passengers. *Cunard Archives – University of Liverpool*

ABOVE The First-class Observation Bar and Cocktail Lounge at the forward end of the *Queen Mary*'s Promenade Deck had a bold red theme, drawing on the Company's colours and reflected throughout in all its fixtures and fittings, most conspicuously the pillars, uplighters and leather upholstery. It included modish red ash trays, the majority of which disappeared on her maiden voyage and are now prized collectibles. *Shawn Drake*

RIGHT Another of the *Queen Elizabeth*'s cocktail bars, this one in Second-class. *Cunard Archives – University of Liverpool*

ABOVE The Café Carinthia on the *Queen Victoria* sits between the Chart Room and the Champagne Bar, at the centre of a sequence of small lounges along the starboard side of Deck 2. Besides beverages and alcoholic drinks, the Café Carinthia serves a range of light snacks and sandwiches. The equivalent area aboard the *Queen Elizabeth* has been re-designated as the Britannia Club, creating an alternative dining room for Britannia-class passengers. *Author*

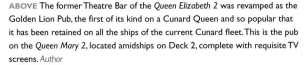

**ABOVE** The former Theatre Bar of the *Queen Elizabeth 2* was revamped as the Golden Lion Pub, the first of its kind on a Cunard Queen and so popular that it has been retained on all the ships of the current Cunard fleet. This is the pub on the *Queen Mary 2*, located amidships on Deck 2, complete with requisite TV screens. *Author*

**ABOVE** Alluding to the Midships Bars of the first two Queens, this is part of the Midships Bar of the new *Queen Elizabeth*, another example of the revival of historic Cunard shipboard locations. Every facet of the décor exhibits references to the *Queen Mary* and *Queen Elizabeth*. *Author*

**ABOVE** The bakery on the *Queen Elizabeth*, revealing some of the heavy-duty electrical appliances necessary for the production of the quantity of bread loaves and rolls that were baked daily. The bakeries aboard Cunard's Queens are the sole department of the kitchens that function on constantly rotating shifts, 24 hours a day every day. *Cunard*

**FAR LEFT** The First-class kitchen of the *Queen Mary*, seen here, is little different to one of the kitchens on the… *Cunard Archives – University of Liverpool*

**LEFT** …later *Queen Victoria* insofar as the ovens, kitchen equipment and general layout are concerned. The one striking difference, in the context of today's greater awareness of health and hygiene risks, is how, on the older ship, there are many inaccessible exposed surfaces, especially on the ventilation ducting and pipework, where dust and grime could have accumulated. *Author*

Sheltered from ocean breezes, this is the Pavilion Pool and surrounding area on the *Queen Victoria* on Deck 9. *Author*

No Jumping or Diving

# Let Us Entertain You

FROM THE PASSENGERS' POINT OF VIEW, given that fine dining and luxurious accommodation have remained constants on Cunard's Queens through to the present, the single aspect of their operation that has seen the greatest improvement has been the range and quality of the offerings for recreational diversion and entertainment.

Back in the days when the *Queen Mary* first entered service, indeed even well into the post-war era when she and the *Queen Elizabeth* were jointly maintaining the regular transatlantic schedules, there was nothing like as much available to amuse and occupy passengers during ocean crossings as there is today.

Much of the entertainment in that period had a self-help feel to it, reminiscent of the audience participation fun that was typical of holiday camps of the time. Unpretentious and light-hearted, it was fare that, at a time when social tastes and attitudes were more innocent and less bothered about sophistication, most found generally acceptable. Strenuous outdoor activity, much as today, was concentrated on deck games and brisk constitutionals around the boat deck which the hardy souls who participated were able to measure into miles because the Company had considerately advised the length of each circuit. In the evenings, there was, and still is, dancing in the ballrooms but overall it was a fairly sedentary ocean lifestyle in the past.

Evening entertainment, and some in the daytime for that matter, to a large extent depended on the inspiration and creativity of members of the ship's crew. Reflecting the lack of priority then given to this dimension of an ocean voyage, there were few dedicated entertainment staff and, strange as it may seem, those personnel who were involved in providing pastimes and diversions for the passengers, including the ship's musicians, were then organised as members of the Deck Department! Horse-racing, or more accurately wagering on the results, in which seamen moved wooden horses along a track or, later, which took the form of projected video recordings, was a particularly popular activity while playing Bingo in the main lounge remained a staple form of recreation well into the service career of the *Queen Elizabeth 2*. Boxing matches could be arranged, usually on the outside deck, if there were willing participants travelling on the ship but they became less common after the early post-war years as pugilism became increasingly viewed as distasteful.

The larger accommodation spaces of the *Queen Mary* and *Queen Elizabeth*, along with those of the other giant 'ships-of-state', allowed the introduction of the first amenities for entertaining passengers as an audience. Apparatus for the showing of 'talkies' was installed aboard the *Queen Mary*, at first in makeshift theatres which were fairly modest affairs with limited seating. In the First-class Main Lounge, a stage was provided at one end although its size limited its use to concerts and recitals. The same room had cine projection apparatus and a film winding room housed at the opposite end at Sun Deck level, above a chair locker, allowing the lounge to be adapted as a cinema with a free-standing screen mounted on the stage. A similar arrangement was adopted for passengers in the lower classes.

ABOVE The First-class cinema of the *Queen Mary* was on her Promenade Deck, added in 1947 in place of the former Starboard Gallery and Deck Pantry. *David Hutchings*

RIGHT Some thirty or more years later, the theatre of the *Queen Elizabeth 2* appears to be little different to that of the *Queen Elizabeth*. The stage has grown slightly but retains the ubiquitous piano suggesting that, despite this being the era of the Swinging Sixties, on-stage entertainment remained fairly formal. She was the first Queen to have a theatre with a balcony, increasing the seating capacity to 530. *Author*

ABOVE Entertainment facilities had moved forward considerably by the time the *Queen Elizabeth* entered service. She had a proper theatre in First-class with tiered seating for an audience of 338 persons. It was a striking auditorium decorated with blue carpet, ivory walls and vermilion seats. Doubling as a cinema, it was one of two on the ship, the other allocated for Third-class use alone. *Cunard Archives – University of Liverpool*

As the constant re-arranging of the Main Lounge furniture was found to be inconvenient and because it was also desired to offer extended film programmes, in alternate showings to First and Second class passengers, the site for a permanent cinema was sought during the *Queen Mary*'s refit at the end of her war service. Her Starboard Gallery, located amidships on the Promenade Deck, which had originally served as a Ballroom Lounge and Smoking Room was selected for the purpose and, combined with part of a Deck Pantry and the starboard side entrance to the Main Lounge, it was turned into a rather narrow but immutable movie facility seating 190 persons. Given that the floor was level, the view for those seated at the back, beneath the projection window must, however, have been very restricted.

Aboard the *Queen Elizabeth*, Cunard-White Star made significant improvements in the entertainment provisions for its passengers. She had a dedicated cinema from new, located at the aft end of the Promenade Deck utilising the space which, aboard the *Queen Mary*, had been the Second-class Smoking Room. Hers was a proper, tiered 338-seat cinema theatre and, as it had a wider and deeper curtained stage, it was possible for the first time, besides the projection of feature films, to put on something that was closer to a recognisable variety show.

The following list provides a flavour of the daily activities which Tourist-class passengers travelling on the *Queen Elizabeth* to Southampton could partake of, in this case on Saturday 18 November 1961:

The day began at 10.00AM with a recorded concert of Dvorak's 'New World Symphony' in the Garden Lounge, followed by the Totalisator on the ship's daily run in the main public rooms for each class. Ray Baines played the Hammond organ in two performances at 11.30AM and 4.45PM while, between them, at 3.45PM, passengers were treated to 'Music for Tea Time' by Tom Peaker and the *Queen Elizabeth* orchestra.

The evening entertainment commenced at 6.00PM with a Cocktail Dance in the Smoke Room but for the more serious-

ABOVE A further quarter of a century on and the elaborate show theatre has arrived aboard the Queens, here on the *Queen Mary 2*. Her Royal Court Theatre rivals anything to be found in the West End or on Broadway, being equipped with dynamic stage and scenery mechanisms, comprehensive lighting systems and balconied seating all round. The theatre's seating capacity is 1,094. *Cunard*

minded there was a broadcast of the BBC News in the Garden Lounge at 6.15PM. Gala Dinner in the Dining Room was followed by a broadcast of 'The Voice of America' and more news at 8.45. The day concluded with Bingo at 9.35PM and dancing until midnight. The day's movie programme comprised a single feature film, 'Back Street' with Susan Hayward and John Gavin, repeated four times.

While the passengers in First and Second-class had their own programme, it consisted of a similar selection of activities as performers moved between the public rooms of each category but virtually nothing took place concurrently allowing passengers anything remotely resembling a choice and the emphasis for all was on music and dancing. Interestingly, the 'Midnight Buffet' (actually from 11.00PM to midnight) served only sandwiches and coffee!

The daily 'Programme for Today' advised passengers to start their preparations for a Fancy Head-Dress Competition which was to be held the following day.

How much that differs from the comprehensive programme of distractions and pastimes, catering for all tastes and interests that is a fundamental feature of today's Queens. Moving forward in time to Sunday, 2 May 2004, aboard the *Queen Mary 2* bound for New York there was an extensive and diverse range of activities, entertainment and amusements for passengers to choose from, starting at 9.00AM.

During the daytime, there were six different Enrichment lectures in either the Illuminations theatre or the Connexions Room, the subjects being The Progress of World War Two – Dunkirk to Alamein, Popular Songs of the 1930s, Jewellery, The Roots of Jazz, Life from the Sea Surface to the Twilight Zone and 'The Arrow of Time'. In the Queen's Room, and at other locations around the ship, classes were available in Line Dancing, Pilates, Bridge, Scarf Tying, Water-colour painting, Samba dancing and Yoga. Musical entertainment comprised a classical concert in Illuminations, jazz in the Chart Room, show music in the Pavilion Bar and piano melodies in the Golden Lion Pub.

The Planetarium in the Illuminations theatre had five afternoon and early evening showings of the feature 'Infinity Express'.

ABOVE The brightly-coloured entrance to Illuminations on the *Queen Mary 2*, has bronze figures and a striking Art Deco influenced carpet pattern. *Cunard*

LEFT The *Queen Mary 2* has a generous provision of entertainment venues. Immediately forward of the Royal Court Theatre's lower level is a second 500-seat theatre, Illuminations, which functions during the day as a lecture hall and planetarium – note the red-seated area reserved for those shows – and as a dedicated cinema at other times. *Cunard*

RIGHT The *Queen Victoria* had the first theatre aboard any passenger ship to have private boxes, a feature retained on the newer *Queen Elizabeth*. The theatre's colour scheme is a bold red, the design having been heavily influenced by the interior of the Victoria Palace Theatre in London. *Author*

FAR RIGHT The shopping arcade of the *Queen Mary*. There were only a few stores, among them a branch of W.H. Smith, the Promenade Shop selling souvenirs and tobacco and a branch of the Midland Bank. Austin Reid of Regent Street's clothing outlet that was in the centre is now called the 'Royal Dragon Emporium'. Concealed lighting in soffits was a feature of the design by Waring and Gillow intended to emphasise the illuminated shop fronts. *Andrew Kilk*

ABOVE Both the *Queen Victoria* and *Queen Elizabeth* have large Royal Court show theatres. That of the *Queen Elizabeth*, shown here, has a plush interior decorated in an old gold and pale blue colour scheme. *Cunard*

Highlights of the evening's programme of events were two performances of 'Rock at the Opera' in the Royal Court Theatre. The day's movie, showing only once at Illuminations at 10.30pm, was 'The Quiet American' starring Michael Caine. There was also Ballroom and Latin Dancing in the Queen's Room, more jazz and piano in the Chart Room and a karaoke in the Golden Lion Pub. All in all, an amazing choice of entertainment and recreational activity!

There have always been VIPs and celebrities of the worlds of entertainment and sport to be found aboard Cunard's Queens but where today they are there specifically to give musical performances, comedy shows or enrichment lectures, in the past they were more likely to be travelling as passengers.

Not only does the modern passenger have a huge choice of pleasurable things to do, but the entertainment, fitness and recreational facilities are outstanding, rivalling the best theatres of the West End or Broadway and the most elaborately equipped sports centres ashore. From working out in a fully-equipped

gymnasium to art and dance classes in the lounge, from golf on an all-weather green to a lecture on wine appreciation, or from a planetarium experience to a full-length song-and-dance theatre show with professional performers, Cunard's modern Queens offer entertainment and recreation that is second to none. And it bears virtually no resemblance to the past!

### ENTERTAINMENT STAFF

The scale of the Entertainment programme is reflected in the much larger entertainment team aboard the *Queen Mary 2*, compared with her predecessors.

| Queen Mary | Queen Elizabeth 2 | Queen Mary 2 |
|---|---|---|
| 30 | 52 | 83 |

NB. The staff on the *Queen Mary* were musicians; on the *QE2* there were also entertainers and dancers but the number stated above, dating from 1986 and possibly increased later, does, however, include 14 Cruise Staff.

**LEFT** The *Queen Mary* was renowned for the size of her First-class Library. The First-class Library on the *Queen Elizabeth*, pictured here, was comparable. One of three such lending libraries on the ship, this triplication of services is, perhaps, a good example of the inefficiency of the class system. Besides books, there was reading matter in the form of the daily newspaper, the 'Ocean Times'. *Cunard*

**RIGHT** There are equally impressive libraries on each of the modern Queens, the *Queen Mary 2*'s carrying some 8,000 titles. The photograph shows the two-level library on the *Queen Victoria*. *Cunard*

**LEFT** Today the Queens' shopping arcades have mainly foreign outlets, Italian, French and American brands being prominent, among them Calvin Klein, Swarovski, H. Stern and others. This is part of the shopping centre of the cruise ship *Queen Elizabeth*, just forward of amidships on Deck 3. *Author*

ABOVE The *Queen Mary 2*'s Canyon Ranch Spa, a 21st-century take on the health spa, offering, among other exotic treatments, a thalassotherapy pool. *Cunard*

LEFT The Second-class inside pool on the *Queen Elizabeth* is well-appointed but rather sterile and unappealing, especially when lacking any sign of human presence as in this stock publicity shot. The *Queen Elizabeth* became the first Cunard Queen to have an outside swimming pool when a Lido Pool was installed aft on her Promenade Deck in the mid-1960s as part of the modifications for cruising. *Cunard Archives – University of Liverpool*

ABOVE For the more fitness-conscious, the Queens have provided excellent exercise and games facilities commencing with the *Queen Mary*. The first two Queens offered a gymnasium, inside swimming pools and a range of Turkish and other health baths comprising tepidarium, calidarium and frigidarium. By the time the *Queen Elizabeth 2* emerged, the vogue was for spas offering much the same selection of health and beauty treatments. This is the *QE2*'s Royal Spa. *Cunard*

ABOVE Swimming pools for those with a constitutional inclination have been a staple provision for the Queens' passengers' recreation. The *Queen Mary* had this ornate, Pompeian pool for her First-class passengers, tiled and decorated in distinctive Art Deco style. *David Hutchings*

**LEFT** Aft on Deck 8, the *Queen Mary 2* has a Terrace Pool with outdoor jacuzzis. Though somewhat incongruous on a cold North Atlantic crossing, they nevertheless allude to the other half of her dual personality – cruising for much of the year in warmer climes. *Cunard*

**RIGHT** The Lido Pool aft on the *Queen Elizabeth*. It is noteworthy that on each of these ships, at both pools, there is plenty of apparatus available to permit disabled passengers to take full advantage of the amenities. *Author*

**LEFT** It is evident that this pool on the *QE2*, one of her two Lido Pools, is first and foremost a place of fun rather than a facility at which certain passengers would pursue a strict, daily exercise routine. *Cunard Archives – University of Liverpool*

**RIGHT** Novel recreational diversions introduced aboard the new *Queen Elizabeth*, housed in the area above her bridge, include a crown green bowling court and a croquet green nearby. *Author*

Sailing into the sunset, the cruise ship *Queen Elizabeth* departs Southampton on her maiden voyage on 12 October 2010. *Author*

# Postscript

IN THE WINTER OF 2008, the *Queen Elizabeth 2* sailed away on her final departure from Southampton, a legend in her time. Two years later, the new *Queen Elizabeth* made her début, once more bringing the modern Queens to three ships and, in so doing, giving Cunard one of the world's youngest cruise passenger fleets, having an average age of just over four years.

So what next? As the Cunard Line advances towards its bicentenary, there will inevitably be new Queens in the future. For some passengers at least, in a world in which heightened terrorism has become a real concern, there is a small but significant demand for an ocean passage in preference to airline travel. With this in mind, there is speculation that Carnival may, at some time soon, commission a sister-ship for the *Queen Mary 2*, possibly for part-time employment on a scheduled service to Australia.

Whether or not that happens, there is no sign of abatement in the appeal of cruise vacations or, more importantly, of the superior cruise experience that Cunard offers on its incomparable Queens.

What is more, there are, too, plenty of names from Britain's royal past and future for Carnival and Cunard to choose from for new Queens: *Queen Catherine, Queen Anne, Queen Boadicea, Queen Jane*…

**RIGHT** The *Queen Elizabeth 2* makes her final departure from her home port Southampton on 11 November 2008 bound for Dubai, a valedictory firework display commemorating the event. *Cunard*

ABOVE The *Queen Elizabeth* looked increasingly unkempt as the 1960s progressed, the heavy losses from the declining
Atlantic scheduled service precluding the high level of maintenance that she had hitherto received. Here, she approaches
Southampton inbound on a misty and murky morning. When it was said of her that "Nothing like her will ever be built again",
it became the catalyst of Stephen Payne's lifelong ambition that resulted in the *Queen Mary 2*. *World Ship Society*

# Queen Mary (1936)

## Career at a Glance

| | |
|---|---|
| Ordered | 28 May 1930 |
| Laid down | 27 December 1930 |
| Builders | John Brown, Clydebank, Scotland |
| Yard Number | 534 |
| Launched | 26 September 1934 (originally planned for February 1932) |
| Patron | HRH Queen Mary |
| Maiden Voyage | 27 May 1936 from Southampton to New York (originally planned for mid-1933) |
| Total Atlantic crossings | 1,001 |
| Total career mileage | 3.6+ million |
| Total career passengers | ca. 2,285,000 |
| War Service | Troopship from May 1940 to September 1946 |
| Total wartime mileage | 569,429 (661,771 total auxiliary mileage) |
| Total wartime passengers | 765,429 (military) 810,730 (total) |
| First commercial voyage after the Second World War | 31 July 1947 from Southampton to New York |
| Final Cunard voyage | 22 September 1967 from New York to Southampton |
| Final sailing | 31 October 1967 from Southampton to Long Beach, California |
| Post-Cunard career | 10 May 1971 to the present, following conversion, as an hotel, museum and convention centre at Long Beach, California |

### Achievements

Atlantic Blue Riband holder: August 1936-March/July 1937 and
  August 1938-July 1952

Highest record average speed: 31.69 knots (36.5 mph)

Largest Cunard passenger ship 1936-1940

First Cunard and British ship to exceed 80,000 grt and 1,000 feet loa

Greatest single complement carried aboard any ship 25-30 July 1943:
  16,683 persons

## Vital Statistics

| | |
|---|---|
| Gross Registered Tonnage | 81,237 |
| Displacement Tonnage | 81,961 |
| Length Overall | 1,019 feet (310.7 metres) |
| Maximum Beam | 119 feet (36.1 metres) |
| Length to Beam ratio | 8.56 |
| Depth (keel to funnel) | 184 feet (56.1 metres) |
| Draught | 39 feet (11.9 metres) |
| Number of passenger decks | 12 |
| Watertight subdivision | 18 bulkheads/160 compartments |
| Main Engines | 16 SR Geared steam turbines |
| Propulsion | Quadruple 4-bladed FP screws |
| Maximum shaft horsepower | 212,000 |
| Trials speed | 32.84 knots (37.82 mph) |
| Service speed | 28.50 knots (32.82 mph) |
| Stabilisers | 2 sets of 2 Denny Brown (retractable) from 1958 |
| Cargo capacity | 44,490 cubic feet |
| Number of classes | 3 |
| Passengers (as built) | 776 Cabin, 784 Tourist, 579 Third |
| Passengers (post-war refit) | 711 First, 707 Cabin, 577 Tourist |
| Passenger/space ratio (post-war) | 40.7 |
| Crew (as built/post-war) | 1,174/1,285 |
| Crew/Passenger ratio | 0.58 |
| Restaurants | 4 |
| Swimming Pools | 2 (inside) |
| Air-conditioning | Partial with forced-air ventilation |
| Port of Registry | Liverpool |
| Radio Call Sign | GBTT |
| LR (IMO) Number | 528793 |

NB: *Some passenger decks include levels which had or have only a single passenger amenity such as an indoor pool, medical centre, sports centre, terrace or spa.*

# Queen Elizabeth (1940)

## Career at a Glance

| | |
|---|---|
| Ordered | 6 October 1936 |
| Laid down | 4 December 1936 |
| Builders | John Brown, Clydebank, Scotland |
| Yard Number | 552 |
| Launched | 27 September 1938 |
| Patron | HRH Queen Elizabeth |
| Maiden Voyage | 2 March 1940 from the River Clyde to New York (originally planned for 27 April 1940) |
| Total Atlantic crossings | 908 |
| Total career mileage | 3,472,672 |
| Total commercial passengers | 2.3 million |
| War Service | Troopship from February 1941 to March 1946 |
| Total wartime mileage | 492,635 |
| Total wartime passengers | 811,324 |
| First commercial voyage after the Second World War | 16 October 1946 from Southampton to New York |
| Final Cunard voyage | 30 October 1968 from New York to Southampton |
| Final sailing | 28 November 1968 from Southampton to Port Everglades, Florida |
| Post-Cunard career | Intended for conversion into an hotel, museum and convention centre at Port Everglades, Florida, under the name Elizabeth. After that scheme failed, sold in August 1970 for conversion into a university cruise ship at Hong Kong, renamed Seawise University. Destroyed by fire at Hong Kong on 9 January 1972. Her remains were removed and broken up over the next three years |

### Achievements

Largest passenger ship in the world: 1940-1997

Longest passenger ship in the world: 1940-1962

Largest Cunard passenger ship: 1940-2003

Fastest ever Cunard passenger ship

## Vital Statistics

| | |
|---|---|
| Gross Registered Tonnage | 83,673 |
| Displacement Tonnage | ca. 83,000 |
| Length Overall | 1,031 feet (313.5 metres) |
| Maximum Beam | 119 feet (36.1 metres) |
| Length to Beam ratio | 8.66 |
| Depth (keel to funnel) | 187 feet (57.0 metres) |
| Draught | 39 feet (11.9 metres) |
| Number of passenger decks | 12 |
| Watertight subdivision | 15 bulkheads/113 compartments |
| Main Engines | 16 SR Geared steam turbines, |
| Propulsion | Quadruple 4-bladed FP screws |
| Maximum shaft horsepower | 212,000 |
| Trials speed | 36.25 knots (41.75 mph) |
| Service speed | 28.50 knots (32.82 mph) |
| Stabilisers | 2 sets of 2 Denny Brown (retractable) from 1955 |
| Cargo capacity | 60,750 cubic feet |
| Number of classes | 3 |
| Passengers (post-war refit) | 823 First, 662 Cabin, 798 Tourist |
| Passengers (1965-1966 refit) | 704 First, 664 Second, 627 Tourist |
| Passenger/space ratio | 36.7 |
| Crew | 1,296 |
| Crew/Passenger ratio | 0.57 |
| Restaurants | 4 |
| Swimming Pools | 2 (inside) outdoor lido pool added 1965 |
| Air-conditioning | Partial (full from 1965) with forced-air ventilation |
| Port of Registry | Liverpool |
| Radio Call Sign | GBSS |
| LR (IMO) Number | 528790 |

# Queen Elizabeth 2 (1969)

## Career at a Glance:

| | |
|---|---|
| Ordered | 30 December 1964 |
| Laid down | 5 July 1965 |
| Builders | John Brown (later Upper Clyde Shipbuilders), Clydebank, Scotland |
| Yard Number | 736 |
| Launched | 20 September 1967 |
| Patron | HM Queen Elizabeth II |
| Maiden Voyage | 2 May 1969 from Southampton to New York |
| | (originally planned for 15 January 1969) |
| Total Atlantic crossings | 803 |
| Total World Cruises | 25 |
| Total career mileage | 5.6 million |
| Total career passengers | 2.5+ million |
| War Service | Troopship from 12 May to 11 June 1982 |
| Total war service mileage | 14,967 |
| Total military passengers | ca. 6,000 |
| First commercial voyage after the Falklands War | 14 August 1982 from Southampton to New York |
| Final Cunard voyage | 27 October 2008 Mediterranean cruise from/to Southampton |
| Final sailing | 11 November 2008 from Southampton to Dubai |
| Post-Cunard career | Laid-up at Dubai pending conversion into a static luxury hotel |

## Achievements

Largest twin-screw passenger ship in the world: 1969-1987

Longest serving Cunard passenger ship at 40 years: 1969-2008

Largest diesel-engined Cunard passenger ship: 1986-2007

First and only ship to travel more than 5.5 million miles

## Vital Statistics

| | |
|---|---|
| Gross Registered Tonnage | 65,863 as built |
| | 70,327 from 1994 |
| Displacement Tonnage | 48,923 (53,453 from 1994) |
| Length Overall | 963 feet (293.5 metres) |
| Maximum Beam | 105 feet (32.0 metres) |
| Length to Beam ratio | 9.17 |
| Depth (keel to funnel) | 171 feet (52.2 metres) |
| Draught | 32.5 feet (9.9 metres) |
| Number of passenger decks | 13 |
| Main Engines (as built) | 4 DR Geared steam turbines |
| Propulsion | Twin 6-bladed FP screws |
| Maximum shaft horsepower | 110,000 |
| Engines (after conversion) | Diesel-electric: 9 MAN/B&W 4-stroke diesels coupled to 2 GEC generators |
| Propulsion | Twin 5-bladed VP screws |
| Maximum shaft horsepower | 129,960 |
| Bow thrusters | 2 Stone Kamewa |
| Trials speed (builders' trials) | 32.46 knots (37.38 mph) |
| Trials speed (conversion trials) | 34.1 knots (39.27 mph) |
| Service speed | 28.5 knots (32.82 mph) |
| Stabilisers | 2 sets of 2 Denny Brown (retractable) |
| Number of classes | 2 |
| Passengers (as built) | 564 First class, 1,441 Tourist class |
| Passengers (as cruise ship) | 1,890 |
| Passenger/space ratio (as cruise ship) | 37.2 |
| Crew | 1,040 |
| Crew/Passenger ratio (as cruise ship | 0.55 |
| Restaurants | 5 |
| Swimming Pools (as built) | 3 (2 outdoor, 1 indoor) |
| Air-conditioning | Full |
| Port of Registry | Southampton |
| Radio Call Sign | GBTT |
| IMO Number | 6725418 |

# Queen Mary 2 (2003)

## Career at a Glance

| | |
|---|---|
| Ordered | 6 November 2000 (10 March 2000*) |
| Laid down | 4 July 2002 |
| Builders | Alstom Chantiers de L'Atlantique (now STX France), St. Nazaire, France |
| Yard Number | G32 |
| Floated | 21 March 2003 |
| Naming Ceremony | 8 January 2004 |
| Patron | HM Queen Elizabeth II |
| Maiden Voyage | 12 January 2004 from Southampton to New York |
| Total Atlantic crossings (to end 2011) | 173 |
| Total World Cruises (to end 2011) | 4 |
| Total career mileage (to Sept. 2008) | 711,288 |
| Total career passengers (to Sept. 2008) | 229,000 |

\* Letter of Intent signed with Chantiers de L'Atlantique: the later date was when the formal contract was signed

## Achievements

Largest passenger ship in the world: 2003-2006

Longest passenger ship in the world: 2003-2010

First Cunard ship to exceed 100,000 grt

Largest Cunard passenger ship: 2003-

## Vital Statistics

| | |
|---|---|
| Gross Registered Tonnage | 148,528 |
| Displacement Tonnage (metric) | 79,461 |
| Length Overall | 1,132 feet (345.0 metres) |
| Maximum Beam | 148 feet (45.0 metres) |
| Length to Beam ratio | 8.38 |
| Depth (keel to funnel) | 236 feet (72.0 metres) |
| Draught | 33 feet (10.1 metres) |
| Number of passenger decks | 13 |
| Watertight subdivision | 41 bulkheads |
| Main Engines | Combined 4 Wartsila diesel and 2 General Electric gas turbine generators (CODAG) |
| Propulsion | Quadruple reversible-motor Rolls-Royce Mermaid propulsion pods (2 fixed, 2 azimuth) with 4-bladed FP screws |
| Maximum engine horsepower | 172,478* |
| Transverse Bow Thrusters | 3 Rolls-Royce with VP propellers |
| Trials speed | ca. 30.00 knots (34.5 mph) |
| Service speed | 28.5 knots (32.82 mph) |
| Stabilisers | 2 sets of 2 Brown Brothers/Rolls-Royce (folding) |
| Number of classes | 1 |
| Passengers | 2,620 |
| Passenger/space ratio | 56.7 |
| Crew | 1,141 (plus concessions staff of 93) |
| Crew/Passenger ratio | 0.48 |
| Restaurants | 8 (Kings Court divides into 4 distinct areas in evenings) |
| Swimming Pools | 3 (outdoor) |
| Air-conditioning | Full: from 6 Carrier centrifugal compressors |
| Port of Registry | Southampton |
| Radio Call Sign | GBQM |
| IMO Number | 9241061 |

\* figure in Lloyds Register – Company figure is 157,000

# Queen Victoria (2007)

## Career at a Glance

| | |
|---|---|
| Ordered | 5 April 2004 |
| Laid down | 12 May 2006 |
| Builders | Fincantieri, Marghera, Italy |
| Yard Number | 6127 |
| Floated | 15 January 2007 |
| Naming Ceremony | 12 December 2007 |
| Patron | HRH Princess of Wales |
| Maiden Cruise | 11 December 2007 from Southampton to Rotterdam |
| Total Atlantic crossings (to end 2011) | 2 |
| Total World Cruises (to end 2011) | 3 |

## Achievements

Largest diesel-engined Cunard passenger ship: 2007-2010
Largest Cunard dedicated cruise ship: 2007-2010

## Vital Statistics

| | |
|---|---|
| Gross Registered Tonnage | 90,049 |
| Displacement Tonnage (metric) | 46,487 |
| Length Overall | 965 feet (293.8 metres) |
| Maximum Beam | 118 feet (36.0 metres) |
| Length to Beam ratio | 9.30 |
| Depth (keel to funnel) | 207 feet (63.0 metres) |
| Draught | 26 feet (7.99 metres) |
| Number of passenger decks | 12 |
| Main Engines | Diesel-electric: Vee-type 4x16 cyl. & 2x12 cyl. Sulzer diesel generators |
| Propulsion | Twin ABB azimuth propulsion pods with 4-bladed FP screws |
| Maximum engine horsepower | 86,146* |
| Transverse Bow Thrusters | 3 with VP propellers |
| Trials speed | 27.0 knots (31.09 mph) |
| Service speed | 23.5 knots (27.06 mph) |
| Stabilisers | 1 set of 2 Fincantieri (folding) |
| Number of classes | 1 |
| Passengers | 2,014 |
| Passenger/space ratio | 44.7 |
| Crew | 992 |
| Crew/Passenger ratio | 0.49 |
| Restaurants | 5 |
| Swimming Pools | 2 (outdoor) |
| Air-conditioning | Full: 4 Carrier centrifugal compressors |
| Port of Registry | Southampton |
| Radio Call Sign | GBQV |
| IMO Number | 9320556 |

* figure in Lloyds Register – Company figure is 84,968

# Queen Elizabeth (2010)

## Career at a Glance

| | |
|---|---|
| Ordered | 10 October 2007 |
| Laid down | 2 July 2009 |
| Builders | Fincantieri, Monfalcone, Italy |
| Yard Number | 6187 |
| Floated | 5 January 2010 |
| Naming Ceremony | 11 October 2010 |
| Patron | HM Queen Elizabeth II |
| Maiden Cruise | 12 October 2010 from Southampton to the Atlantic Isles |
| Total Atlantic crossings (to end 2011) | 2 |
| Total World Cruises (to end 2011) | 1 |

### Achievements

Largest diesel-engined Cunard passenger ship: 2010-
Largest Cunard dedicated cruise ship: 2010-

## Vital Statistics

| | |
|---|---|
| Gross Registered Tonnage | 90,901 |
| Displacement Tonnage (metric) | 47,263 |
| Length Overall | 965 feet (293.8 metres) |
| Maximum Beam | 118 feet (36.0 metres) |
| Length to Beam ratio | 9.30 |
| Depth (keel to funnel) | 207 feet (63.1 metres) |
| Draught | 26 feet (7.99 metres) |
| Number of passenger decks | 12 |
| Main Engines | Diesel-electric: 4x12 cyl. Vee-type & 2x8 cyl. inline-type MAK diesel generators |
| Propulsion | Twin ABB azimuth propulsion pods with 4-bladed FP screws |
| Maximum engine horsepower | 84,967* |
| Transverse Bow Thrusters | 3 with VP propellers |
| Trials speed | 27.0 knots (31.09 mph) |
| Service speed | 23.5 knots (27.06 mph) |
| Stabilisers | 1 set of 2 Fincantieri (folding) |
| Number of classes | 1 |
| Passengers | 2,058 |
| Passenger/space ratio | 44.2 |
| Crew | 1,005 |
| Crew/Passenger ratio | 0.49 |
| Restaurants | 5 |
| Swimming Pools | 2 (outdoor) |
| Air-conditioning | Full: 4 Carrier centrifugal compressors |
| Port of Registry | Southampton |
| Radio Call Sign | GBTT |
| IMO Number | 9477438 |

* Company figure.

# Bibliography

Ellery, David *RMS Queen Mary* (Conway Maritime Press, 2006)

Hutchings, David *Pride of the North Atlantic* (Kingfisher Publications, 2003)

de Kerbrech, Richard & Williams, David, *Damned by Destiny* (Teredo Books, 1982)

Maxtone-Graham, John *The North Atlantic Run* (Cassell, 1972) *Liners to the Sun* (Macmillan, 1985)

Philips-Burt, Douglas *When Luxury Went to Sea* (David & Charles, 1971)

Potter, Neil & Frost, Jack *The Mary – The Inevitable Ship* (Harrap, 1961) *The Elizabeth* (Harrap, 1965)

Ransome-Wallis, P. *The Sea and Ships* (Ian Allan, c. 1956)

Steele, James *Queen Mary* (Phaidon, 1995)

Wealleans, Anne *Designing Liners* (Routledge, 2006)

Williams, David *Cunard's Legendary Queens of the Seas* (Ian Allan, 2004) *Glory Days: Cunard* (Ian Allan, 1998) *Sea Traffic Management* (Ian Allan, 1988)

Winter, C.W. Ron *Queen Mary, Her Early Years Recalled* (Forget-Me-Not Books, 1993)

Special Supplements & Articles:

*Institute of Marine Engineering, Science & Technology* 'The Evolution of a Queen' (Marine Engineers Review, 2004)

*Lloyd's List* 'Compass to ARPA: Navigation Down the Years' and 'From Signal Station to Satellite' (1984)

*The Naval Architect* 'Genesis of a Queen' (2004)

'Science at Sea' by Raymond Blackman *Modern World Book of Ships*, c1950

'Wireless at Sea' by Harold Golding *The Wonder Book of Ships*, c1932)

# *Acknowledgements*

I would like to record my appreciation of the assistance in the preparation of this book that I received from the following individuals and organisations:

From Cunard Line & Carnival Corporation my particular gratitude goes to Michael Gallagher for permission to reproduce many of the Company's photographs and for his help with countless requests for technical information and other ship details, and to Christina Hannon for arranging and escorting me on ship visits to permit me to conduct interviews and take photographs; also to Frank Prowse, Director Fleet Personnel, Cunard Line Hotel & Entertainment. I would also like to mention the valuable help received from Operations shore personnel Corrine Batty, Liam Taylor, Maureen Glasspool and Gregory Dorothy. And, above all, I would like to thank Peter Shanks, Cunard Line's President and Managing Director, for kindly writing the Foreword.

Valuable contributions, in the form of anecdotes, quotations (some from Beyondships.com) and technical data, from the following former and present Cunard personnel are gratefully acknowledged: Brian Atkinson (Chief Mechanical Engineer, *Queen Elizabeth 2*) , Chris Bancroft (Able Seaman, *Queen Mary* and *Queen Elizabeth*), Udo Bleeck (MAN Representative aboard *Queen Elizabeth 2*), John Duffy (Hotel Manager, *Queen Mary 2*), Jamie Firth (Britannia Restaurant Maitre d', *Queen Mary 2*), Jean-Marie Zimmerman (Cunard World Culinary Ambassador), Jonathan Norton (Princess Grill Manager and Hotel Manager's Assistant, *Queen Elizabeth 2*), Paul O'Loughlin (Entertainment Director, *Queen Mary 2*), Mervyn Pearsòn (Engineer, *Queen Mary*), Philip Rentell (Junior Second Officer, *Queen Elizabeth 2*), Roland Sarguran (Executive Sous Chef, *Queen Victoria*), Brian Watling (Chief Engineer, *Queen Mary 2*) and the late Ron [CWR] Winter (Junior Electrical Engineer, *Queen Mary*). I would like to record my particular thanks to Bernhard Stumpfel, the Executive Chef on *Queen Victoria*, with whom I had a most informative and entertaining interview.

My sincere thanks go to Shawn Drake who, at my request, kindly took new photographs of details aboard the *Queen Mary* at Long Beach, to Mariane Fricker and the late Phil Fricker, to David Hutchings, an authority on the first three Queens, to Andrew Kilk for his kind help despite illness, to Mick Lindsay and Bert Moody, and to Jim McFaul of the World Ship Society. I would like to single out for particular mention my friend and colleague Richard de Kerbrech for his support and contributions to the project and for kindly, though unofficially, proof-reading the technical sections, helping to clarify a number of engineering and navigational points.

I would also like to thank the following organisations and institutions, and their representatives where noted, for their support or assistance with pictures and information:

Alstom – Chantiers de L'Atlantique [now STX-France] (Bernard Biger)
Cruise & Passenger Services (Nigel Graham)
Fincantieri (Antonio Autorino and Gianfranco Gulli)
National Archives of Scotland (Gillian Mapstone and Robin Urquhart)
Ocean Bookshop (Rebecca Money and Kerry Spencer)
Open Agency (Emma Bacon)
Red Funnel Group (Tom Pell-Stevens)
Southampton Cultural Services
University of Liverpool, Cunard Archives (Dr. Maureen Watry, Katherine Ankers and Heather Anderson)